# Italian

## BIBLE

# Italian

## BIBLE

Rachael Lane

# Contents

Introduction

Italians eat as they live, passionately and with gusto. They take great pleasure in their food and in the company they share it with. Friends and family gather to prepare the feast together, sharing stories and debating who has the best gnocchi recipe! The generosity of the Italian table is evident, with meals often three or more courses and stretching on for hours.

Traditional meals begin with a selection of starters (*antipasto*), followed by a small helping of pasta, risotto or a fresh seasonal soup. Fish, meat or poultry, braised and roasted, are served next. A side dish of vegetables or salad, known as the *contorno*, always accompanies the main meal. And finally is the *dolce* or dessert.

This book covers a broad range of traditional-style Italian fare. Gathered from regions across the country, a wide selection of produce, flavours and cooking techniques are used. The recipes are designed to create a satisfying meal on their own or can form part of an Italian feast, to be shared with family and friends.

# Italian Basics

Italian flavours are simple, with the emphasis on local ingredients. Vegetables are home-grown or sourced fresh from marketplaces and produce is used seasonally when flavours are at their best.

## The Ingredients

A great deal of care is taken to use quality products. Bread is baked daily. Meats are cured and made into salami, bresaola, pancetta, prosciutto, parma and coppa. Olives are preserved, marinated, stuffed and pressed into oil. Vine-ripened tomatoes are sun-dried or cooked down to make rich pasta sauces and soups. Anchovies are dried and preserved in salt and oil. Ricotta and buffalo mozzarella are made fresh on a daily basis. And cheeses like parmesan, pecorino and fontina are found in many dishes. Pasta – fresh, dried and filled – is ever-present in Italian households. Decadent sweets and pastries are flavoured with nuts, liqueurs, chocolate and citrus. And of course at the end of every meal a digestive such as grappa or limoncello is served, followed by an espresso.

## Regional Influences

The food of Italy changes from region to region, with each having its own speciality. In the North, the terrain is mountainous with a cooler climate. Short-grain rice such as arborio is grown here, packaged and sold as risotto. However, the land is better suited to grazing than to growing crops. Veal, beef and pork are reared, and used to produce spicy sausages, salami and other cured meats. Warm nourishing dishes such as slow-cooked and braised meats, thick polenta and hearty broths come from this region.

In the South, the climate is hotter and the food tends to be lighter. Tomatoes, olives, capsicums, eggplants, arti-chokes, garlic, oranges, lemons and nuts are grown here. Fish and seafood such as tuna, swordfish, sea bream, sea bass, squid, oysters, mussels and clams are in abundant supply and can be found on most menus. Dried fruits and fresh herbs such as rosemary, basil, parsley, mint, fennel and oregano are used to flavour dishes.

## The Italian Kitchen

There are a few essential items used in the pasta recipes including a large pasta pot, slotted spoon, and fluted dough wheel (though this can easily be replaced with a sharp knife). Other recipes call for 25-cm (10-in) pizza trays, cannoli tubes, a pastry bag and piping nozzles. All are available from kitchenware stores.

If you plan to make homemade pasta, the most useful piece of equipment is a pasta machine. There are numerous varieties available, most reasonably inexpensive to buy, and they will knead, roll and even cut the dough for you. Always brush out any excess flour after use and store in a clean, dry place. (Never wash your pasta machine, it will cause it to rust.)

# Starters

A traditional Italian meal begins with the antipasto – a selection of hot and cold appetisers shared amongst guests. Most of the starters that follow can be offered as antipasti.

If preparing one or two dishes only, team them with some cured meats, cheese and crostini.

< Stuffed Mussels (page 8)

# Stuffed Mussels

Serves 4–6

1 kg (2 lb 3 oz) black mussels

½ cup (125 ml/4 fl oz) dry white wine

1 tablespoon (20 ml/¾ fl oz) olive oil

½ small onion, finely diced

1 garlic clove, finely chopped

2 anchovy fillets, finely chopped

2 tablespoons finely chopped parsley

2 tablespoons finely chopped oregano

1 teaspoon finely grated lemon zest

1 cup breadcrumbs, made from day-old country-style bread

salt and freshly ground black pepper

extra-virgin olive oil, to serve

Preheat the oven to 200°C (390°F).

Scrub the mussels, discarding any shells that remain open. Remove the beards and rinse clean.

Place the mussels and wine in a large saucepan over high heat. Cover and cook for 4–5 minutes, until opened. (Discard any unopened mussels.) Arrange mussels, in the half shell, in a single layer on a baking tray.

Heat the oil in a frying pan over low–medium heat. Add the onion and garlic and sauté until softened. Add the anchovies and sauté for a further minute, until dissolved. Stir in the parsley, oregano, lemon zest and breadcrumbs. Season with salt and pepper.

Sprinkle the crumb mixture over the mussels to cover. Drizzle with extra-virgin olive oil and bake in the oven for 10 minutes, until golden-brown.

# Fried Whitebait

Serves 4–6

olive oil, for deep-frying

¾ cup (125 g/4½ oz) plain
flour

salt and freshly ground black
pepper

500 g (1 lb 2 oz) whitebait

1 lemon, cut into wedges

Half-fill a heavy-based saucepan with oil. Heat the oil to 180°C (350°F) or until a piece of bread browns in 15 seconds when tested.

Place the flour in a small bowl and season with salt and pepper. Dry the whitebait using paper towel and toss it in the flour, shaking off any excess. Fry the whitebait in batches for 4–5 minutes, turning occasionally until crisp and golden-brown. Remove using a slotted spoon and drain on paper towel. Season with salt.

Serve with lemon wedges.

# Zucchini Frittata

Serves 6

2 tablespoons (40 ml/1½ fl oz) olive oil

1 small onion, finely sliced

2 cloves garlic, finely chopped

3 small zucchini, trimmed and thinly sliced

8 large eggs, lightly beaten

125 g (4 oz) ricotta, crumbled

½ cup shaved salted ricotta

3 tablespoons finely chopped mint

salt and freshly ground black pepper

Preheat grill to medium–high.

Heat the oil in a 23-cm (9-in) ovenproof frying pan over low–medium heat. Add the onion and garlic and sauté until softened. Add the zucchini and sauté for 4–6 minutes, until golden-brown.

Spread the zucchini evenly over the base of the pan and pour in the egg mixture. Scatter the ricotta, salted ricotta and mint over the top. Season with salt and pepper and cook for 5–8 minutes over low–medium heat, until almost set. Place pan under the grill and cook for a further 2 minutes, until the cheese has melted and frittata is completely set.

Slice into portions. Serve warm or at room temperature.

# Tomato, Basil & Mozzarella Bruschetta

Serves 4

2 medium vine-ripened
  tomatoes, diced

½ cup basil leaves, torn

1 ball buffalo mozzarella, torn

4 tablespoons (80 ml/3 fl oz)
  extra-virgin olive oil

salt and freshly ground black
  pepper

4 thin slices country-style
  bread

1 clove garlic, halved

Preheat grill to medium–high.

Place the tomato, basil and mozzarella in a medium bowl. Add 1 table-spoon of the oil and season with salt and pepper, and toss to combine.

Grill the bread until golden-brown. Rub the garlic over the bread on one side and drizzle with olive oil. Top the bread with the tomato mixture and serve immediately.

# Carpaccio

Serves 4

300 g (10 oz) beef fillet

¼ cup thinly shaved parmesan, to serve

freshly ground black pepper

MAYONNAISE

1 large egg yolk

1 tablespoon red-wine vinegar

1 teaspoon Dijon mustard

½ clove garlic, crushed

½ cup (125 ml/4 fl oz) olive oil

salt and freshly ground black pepper

Place four serving plates in the refrigerator to chill until required.

Trim the beef removing any fat or sinew. Tightly wrap the beef in several layers of cling wrap, creating a round shape and covering the meat entirely. Place in the freezer for 45–60 minutes, until firm, but not frozen.

Meanwhile to make the mayonnaise, combine the egg yolk, vinegar, mustard and garlic together in a medium-sized bowl. Gradually add the oil in a thin stream, whisking continuously until thick and creamy. Season with salt and pepper.

Unwrap the beef and cut wafer-thin slices using a very sharp knife. Arrange the slices on the chilled plates as you go, with slices overlapping slightly. Drizzle with mayonnaise, scatter with parmesan and season with pepper.

# Sardines with Raisins & Pine Nuts

Serves 4

800 g (1 lb 12 oz) sardines,
scaled, cleaned and boned

2 tablespoons (40 ml/1½ fl oz)
extra-virgin olive oil

FILLING

⅔ cup coarsely chopped
breadcrumbs, made from
day-old country-style bread

2 tablespoons (40 ml/1½ fl oz)
extra-virgin olive oil

2 tablespoons raisins

2 tablespoons pine nuts,
lightly toasted

2 tablespoons finely grated
parmesan

1 tablespoon finely chopped
flat-leaf parsley leaves

1 tablespoon finely chopped
rosemary

1 tablespoon (20 ml/¾ fl oz)
lemon juice

1 clove garlic, finely chopped

salt and freshly ground black
pepper

Preheat the oven to 160°C (320°F).

To make filling, place the breadcrumbs on a baking tray and drizzle with the oil. Bake in the oven for 10–15 minutes, until golden-brown. Finely chop and set aside.

Increase the oven temperature to 200°C (390°F). Lightly oil a baking dish.

Combine the breadcrumbs, raisins, pine nuts, parmesan, parsley, rosemary, lemon juice and garlic in a small bowl. Season with salt and pepper.

Spoon the filling into the sardine cavities and arrange the sardines on the baking dish in a single layer. Drizzle with the olive oil and bake in the oven for 10–15 minutes, until golden-brown.

Serve warm or at room temperature.

# Baked Eggplant & Ricotta Rolls

Serves 4

2 medium, long eggplants

4 tablespoons (80 ml/3 fl oz) olive oil

400 g (14 oz) fresh firm ricotta

1 cup grated pecorino

2 tablespoons finely chopped basil

2 tablespoons finely chopped oregano

2 tablespoons finely chopped thyme

¼ cup basil pesto

TOMATO SAUCE

2 tablespoons (40 ml/1½ fl oz) extra-virgin olive oil

1 small onion, diced

1 clove garlic, finely chopped

1 × 410-g (14½-oz) can crushed tomatoes

1 tablespoon tomato paste

½ teaspoon sugar

salt and freshly ground black pepper

Preheat the oven to 200°C (390°F).

To make the sauce, heat the oil in a heavy-based saucepan over low–medium heat. Add the onion and garlic and sauté until softened. Add the tomatoes, tomato paste and sugar and bring to the boil. Decrease the heat to low and gently simmer for 20 minutes. Remove from the heat and let cool slightly. Pour into a food processor and blend until puréed. Season with salt and pepper. >

Cut the eggplants lengthways into thin slices.

Heat half of the oil in a large, non-stick frying pan over medium heat. Grill half of the eggplant slices for 2 minutes on each side, until golden-brown. Repeat with the remaining oil and eggplant.

Combine the ricotta with half of the pecorino, the basil, oregano and thyme in a medium bowl. Season with salt and pepper. Spread over the eggplant slices and roll up lengthways.

Spoon one third of the sauce into a small baking dish. Arrange the eggplant rolls, seam side down, in the dish and cover with the remaining sauce. Scatter spoonfuls of pesto over the top and sprinkle with remaining pecorino. Cover with aluminium foil and bake in the oven for 20 minutes. Uncover and bake for a further 5–10 minutes, until cheese is golden-brown.

# Fried Zucchini Flowers

Serves 4

12 zucchini flowers with baby
zucchini attached

⅓ cup (50 g/1¾ oz) plain flour

¾ cup (180 ml/6 fl oz) water

vegetable oil, for deep-frying

FILLING

50 g (1¾ oz) ricotta cheese

50 g (1¾ oz) soft goat's cheese

1 tablespoon grated parmesan

1 tablespoon finely chopped
basil

1 tablespoon finely chopped
mint

½ teaspoon finely grated
lemon zest

salt and freshly ground black
pepper

Combine the ricotta, goat's cheese, parmesan, basil, mint and lemon zest in a bowl. Season with salt and pepper. Gently open the zucchini flowers and spoon a heaped teaspoon of the mixture inside. Close to encase the filling.

Combine the flour and water in a bowl, stirring to make a smooth batter.

Half-fill a large, heavy-based saucepan with oil for deep-frying. Heat the oil to 180°C (350°F) or until a piece of bread browns in 15 seconds. Dip the flowers in batter and fry in batches, turning occasionally, for 3–4 minutes, until crisp and golden-brown. Remove using a slotted spoon and drain on paper towel. Season with salt.

# Roasted Capsicum, Basil & Fontina Arancini

Serves 6

80 g (3 oz) butter

1 tablespoon (20 ml/¾ fl oz) olive oil

1 small onion, finely chopped

2 cloves garlic, finely chopped

1 cup (200 g/7 oz) arborio rice

½ cup (125 ml/4 fl oz) dry white wine

3½ cups (875 ml/29½ fl oz) vegetable stock, heated

2 roasted red capsicums, finely chopped

½ cup grated parmesan

1 cup finely chopped basil leaves

salt and freshly ground black pepper

150 g (5 oz) fontina cheese, cut into cubes

⅓ cup (50 g/1¾ oz) plain flour

2 large eggs, lightly beaten

⅔ cup fine dry breadcrumbs

vegetable oil, for deep-frying

Heat half of the butter and the oil in a large, heavy-based saucepan over low–medium heat. Add the onion and garlic and sauté until softened. Add the rice, stirring to coat, and cook for 2 minutes, until translucent.

Pour in the wine and stir until all the liquid has been absorbed. Gradually add the stock, a ladle at a time. Ensure all the liquid is absorbed before the next addition. Cook for 20–25 minutes, stirring constantly, until all the liquid has been added and absorbed. The rice should be tender and cooked. Stir in the capsicum, parmesan, basil and the remaining butter. Season to taste. >

Line a tray with baking paper and spread the risotto over. Set aside to cool.

Shape cooled risotto into balls the size of a small orange (*arancini* in Italian). Make a hole in each ball with your finger and insert a cube of fontina. Reshape ball to enclose cheese. Crumb the arancini, rolling each one in flour, followed by the egg and then the crumbs.

Half-fill a large heavy-based saucepan with oil. Heat the oil to 180°C (360°F) or until a piece of bread browns in 15 seconds when tested.

Fry the arancini in batches for 4–5 minutes, turning occasionally, until golden-brown. Remove using a slotted spoon and drain on paper towel. Season with salt.

Serve warm or at room temperature.

# Stuffed Olives

Makes 40 (serves 8–10)

40 large green olives, such as gordal, pitted

½ cup (75 g/2½ oz) plain flour

2 large eggs, lightly beaten

1½ cups bread crumbs, made from day-old country-style bread

olive oil, for deep-frying

FILLING

125 g (4½ oz) veal mince

125 g (4½ oz) pork mince

2 tablespoons finely grated parmesan

2 tablespoons finely grated provolone

2 tablespoons finely diced onion

1 teaspoon finely chopped rosemary

½ clove garlic, finely chopped

½ teaspoon finely grated lemon zest

salt and freshly ground black pepper

To make the filling, combine all of the ingredients together in a medium bowl. Season with salt and pepper. Spoon the filling into a pastry bag fitted with a small plain nozzle and pipe into the olives.

Crumb the olives, rolling each one in flour, followed by egg and then crumbs. Half-fill a heavy-based saucepan with oil. Heat the oil to 180°C (350°F) or until a piece of bread browns in 15 seconds when tested. Fry the olives in batches for 2–3 minutes, turning occasionally, until golden-brown. Remove using a slotted spoon and drain on paper towel.

# Soups

Italian soups vary from delicate broths such as stracciatella, to hearty vegetable, bean and pasta-filled soups, such as the well-known minestrone.

Often accompanied with crusty bread, soups can stand alone to make a satisfying meal, or can be served as the first course of a traditional Italian meal. Always use homemade or quality stock for best results.

< Fennel, Tomato & Sausage Soup (page 28)

# Fennel, Tomato & Sausage Soup

Serves 4

4 tablespoons (80 ml/3 fl oz)
olive oil

4 spicy Italian sausages,
casings removed and
meat sliced

75 g (2½ oz) diced pancetta

1 large onion, diced

3 cloves garlic, sliced

2 bay leaves

8 sprigs thyme

1 large fennel bulb, trimmed
and thinly sliced

1 teaspoon soft brown sugar

1.5 kg (3 lb 5 oz) roma
tomatoes, coarsely chopped

1 L (34 fl oz) chicken stock

salt and freshly ground black
pepper

Heat half of the oil in a heavy-based saucepan over medium–high heat.
Add the sausage meat and pancetta and cook until browned. Transfer to a
plate and set aside.

Heat the remaining oil in the pan over low–medium heat. Add the onion,
garlic, bay leaves and thyme, and sauté until golden. Add the fennel and
sauté for 5 minutes, until just softened. Add the brown sugar and sauté,
stirring, for a further 5 minutes, until golden-brown. Return the sausage
and pancetta to the pan. Add the tomatoes and stock and bring to the boil.
Decrease the heat and gently simmer for 20–30 minutes. Season with salt
and pepper.

# Minestrone

Serves 4–6

2 tablespoons (40 ml/1½ fl oz) olive oil

1 medium onion, diced

50 g (1¾ oz) pancetta, finely chopped

2 cloves garlic, finely chopped

1 stick celery, diced

1 medium carrot, diced

2 medium potatoes, peeled and diced

1 bay leaf

1 cup (250 ml/8½ fl oz) passata

2 tablespoons tomato paste

1.25 L (2 pt 10 fl oz) chicken or vegetable stock

1 × 400-g (14-oz) can borlotti beans, drained and rinsed

1 cup small pasta shapes

1 medium zucchini, diced

¼ savoy cabbage, chopped

¼ cup chopped flat-leaf parsley

salt and freshly ground pepper

extra-virgin olive oil, to serve

grated parmesan, to serve

Heat the oil in a large, heavy-based saucepan over low–medium heat. Add the onion, pancetta and garlic and sauté until golden. Add celery, carrot and potato and cook for 3–4 minutes, until they begin to colour. Add the bay leaf, passata, tomato paste and stock and bring to the boil. Add the beans, pasta, zucchini and cabbage, decrease the heat to low and gently simmer for 30–35 minutes, until the pasta and vegetables are cooked. Stir in the parsley and season with salt and pepper.

Serve drizzled with oil and scattered with parmesan.

# Pasta & Bean Soup

Pasta e fagioli

Serves 6

300 g (10½ oz) dried
cannellini beans, soaked in
cold water overnight

1 tablespoon salt

3 tablespoons (60 ml/2 fl oz)
olive oil

1 medium onion, finely
chopped

1 stick celery, finely chopped

2 cloves garlic, finely chopped

2 bay leaves

200 g (7 oz) pancetta, diced

1.25 L (2 pt 10 fl oz) chicken
or vegetable stock

1½ cups (375 ml/12½ fl oz)
passata

juice of ½ lemon

150 g (5 oz) pappardelle,
broken into shorter lengths

¼ cup chopped flat-leaf parsley

salt and freshly ground pepper

extra-virgin olive oil, to serve

Bring a large saucepan of water to the boil. Add the drained beans, decrease the heat and gently simmer. Cook for 30 minutes. Add salt and cook for a further 30 minutes, until beans are al dente. Drain and set aside.

Heat the oil in a large saucepan over low–medium heat. Add the onion, celery, garlic and bay leaves and sauté until softened. Add the pancetta and cook for a further 3–5 minutes, until golden. Add the beans, stock, passata and lemon juice and bring to the boil. Add the pasta and cook for 10 minutes, until al dente. Stir in the parsley and season with salt and pepper.

# Mussel & Clam Soup

## Zuppa di cozze e vongole

Serves 6

500 g (1 lb 2 oz) black mussels

500 g (1 lb 2 oz) clams

4 medium vine-ripened tomatoes, blanched and peeled

3 tablespoons (60 ml/2 fl oz) extra-virgin olive oil

1 small onion, finely chopped

2 cloves garlic, finely chopped

½ cup (125 ml/4 fl oz) dry white wine

1½ cups (375 ml/12½ fl oz) fish stock

¼ cup finely chopped flat-leaf parsley

20 g butter, diced

salt and freshly ground black pepper

4 slices ciabatta bread, toasted

Scrub the mussels and clams clean, discarding any shells that remain open. Beard the mussels and rinse clean.

Cut the tomatoes into quarters. Scrape out the seeds and discard. Dice the flesh and set aside.

Heat the oil in a medium, heavy-based saucepan over low–medium heat. Add the onion and garlic, and sauté until softened. Pour in the wine and cook until reduced by half. Pour in the stock and bring to the boil. Decrease the heat and gently simmer for 10 minutes.

Add the tomatoes, mussels and clams. Cover and cook for 5 minutes, until shellfish have opened. (Discard any unopened shells.) Add the parsley and butter and toss to coat. Season with salt and pepper.

To serve, place a slice of bread in the bottom of each bowl and ladle the soup over.

# Re-boiled Soup

## Ribollita

Serves 4–6

4 medium vine-ripened tomatoes, blanched and peeled

4 tablespoons (80 ml/3 fl oz) olive oil

1 medium red onion, diced

1 leek, white part only, coarsely chopped

2 cloves garlic, finely chopped

2 sticks celery, diced

1 medium carrot, diced

1 medium potato, peeled and diced

1 × 400-g (14-oz) can cannellini beans, rinsed and drained

300 g (10½ oz) cavolo nero, stalks trimmed and leaves finely chopped

1.25 L (2 pt 10 fl oz) chicken stock

4 slices day-old ciabatta bread, to serve

grated parmesan, to serve

extra-virgin olive oil, to serve

Coarsely chop the tomatoes and set aside.

Heat 3 tablespoons of the oil in a large, heavy-based saucepan over low–medium heat. Add the onion, leek and garlic, and sauté until softened. Add the celery, carrot and potato, and cook for 5 minutes. >

Add the tomato, beans and cavolo nero. Pour in the stock and bring to the boil. Decrease the heat to low, and gently simmer for 1–1½ hours, until the vegetables begin to fall apart.

Meanwhile preheat grill to medium. Brush the bread with the remaining oil and grill until golden-brown.

To serve, place a slice of bread in the bottom of each bowl and ladle the soup over. Top with parmesan and drizzle with oil.

# Stracciatella

Serves 6

2 L (4 pt 4 fl oz) chicken or
  beef stock

½ cup (80 g/3 oz) risoni

salt and freshly ground black
  pepper

4 large eggs, lightly beaten

4 tablespoons grated parmesan

¼ cup finely chopped flat-leaf
  parsley

Place the stock in a medium saucepan over medium–high heat and bring
to the boil. Add the risoni and cook for 10 minutes, until al dente. Season
with salt and pepper.

Pour the egg mixture into the soup in a thin stream, creating thin strands of
cooked egg. Cook for a further 1–2 minutes.

Serve sprinkled with parmesan and parsley.

# Wild Mushroom Soup

Serves 4

300 g (10½ oz) assorted wild mushrooms, sliced if large

4 leaves cavolo nero, finely shredded

salt and freshly ground black pepper

extra-virgin olive oil, to serve

MUSHROOM STOCK

1 small onion, coarsely chopped

1 small carrot, coarsely chopped

2 sticks celery, coarsely chopped

30 g (1 oz) dried porcini mushrooms

2 bay leaves

4 parsley stalks

3 sprigs thyme

3 strips lemon zest

3 black peppercorns

1 clove garlic, crushed

1.5 L (3 pt 3 fl oz) water

To make the mushroom stock, place all the ingredients in a large pot over medium–high heat and bring to the boil. Decrease the heat to low and gently simmer for 2 hours, until the flavour is well-developed. Strain through a fine mesh sieve into a medium saucepan.

Add the mushrooms and cavolo nero to the pan and gently simmer for 5–10 minutes, until tender. Season with salt and pepper.

Serve drizzled with oil.

# Potato & Roast Garlic Soup

Serves 4

4 garlic bulbs

3 tablespoons (60 ml/2 fl oz) olive oil

1 medium onion, diced

3 tablespoons finely chopped thyme

2 bay leaves

3 medium potatoes, peeled and diced

1.25 L (2 pt 10 fl oz) chicken or vegetable stock

salt and freshly ground black pepper

white truffle oil, to serve

Preheat the oven to 180°C (360°F).

Wrap the garlic bulbs in aluminium foil and bake in the oven for 20–25 minutes. Remove from the oven and pinch off skin when cooled.

Heat the oil in a large, heavy-based saucepan over low–medium heat. Add the onion, thyme and bay leaves, and sauté until softened. Add the potatoes and stir for 3–4 minutes. Pour in the stock and bring to the boil. Decrease heat to low, add garlic and gently simmer for 30–35 minutes, until potato is tender.

Remove from heat and leave to cool slightly. Using a food processor, purée until smooth. Return to the pan and reheat if necessary. Season with salt.

Serve with a drizzle of white truffle oil and freshly ground black pepper.

# Tomato & Bread Soup

## Pappa al pomodoro

Serves 4

625 g (1 lb 6 oz) vine-ripened tomatoes, blanched and peeled

2 tablespoons (40 ml/1½ fl oz) olive oil

1 small onion, finely diced

1 clove garlic, finely chopped

1 stick celery, finely diced

1 L (2 pt 10 fl oz) chicken or vegetable stock

2 thick slices day-old ciabatta bread, crusts removed and cubed

salt and freshly ground black pepper

3 tablespoons finely chopped basil

shaved parmesan, to serve

Chop the tomatoes coarsely and set aside.

Heat the oil in a medium, heavy-based saucepan over low–medium heat. Add the onion, garlic and celery, and sauté until softened. Add the tomatoes and stock, and bring to the boil. Decrease the heat to low and gently simmer for 30 minutes. Add the bread, cover and cook for a further 10 minutes, until thickened. Season with salt and pepper.

Serve sprinkled with basil and parmesan.

# Pea & Fennel Soup

Serves 4

3 medium fennel bulbs

3 tablespoons (60 ml/2 fl oz) olive oil

1 large onion, finely sliced

1.25 L (3 pt 3 fl oz) chicken stock

500 g (1 lb 2 oz) frozen peas

3 tablespoons chopped dill

salt and freshly ground black pepper

4 thin slices salted ricotta

extra-virgin olive oil, to serve

Remove and discard the tough outer layers of the fennel. Cut bulbs in half lengthways, remove the hard core, then finely slice.

Heat the oil in a heavy-based saucepan over low–medium heat. Add the onion and sauté until softened. Add the fennel and sauté for a further 5 minutes. Pour in the stock and bring to the boil. Decrease the heat to low and gently simmer for 20–25 minutes, until fennel is tender. Add the peas and cook for a further 5 minutes. Stir in the dill and season with salt and pepper.

Serve topped with salted ricotta and a drizzle of extra-virgin olive oil.

# Pasta & Risotto

In Italy, pasta and risotto are traditionally served as the *primo piatto* or 'first plate'. The flavours are kept simple and a bowl of parmesan is always close at hand. Both pasta and risotto are highly adaptable and dishes require only a handful of ingredients. Always use quality stock, olive oil and cheeses for the best outcome. Pasta and risotto should be cooked until al dente – soft on the outside but still slightly firm to the tooth.

Fresh pasta is not necessarily superior to dried, nor is one variety better than another. Flat and thin pastas are designed to be coated in thinner sauces, whereas pasta shapes are designed to hold thicker sauces in their holes and ridges. Pastas with a rough surface will grip the sauce better than those with a smooth surface.

For best results cook pasta in a large pot of rapidly boiling salted water. (The pasta should be able to move around freely, to prevent sticking.)

< Fresh Egg Pasta (page 48)

# Rolling and Cutting Homemade Pasta

**Pasta sheets** Divide the prepared dough into quarters. Lightly flour the bench and shape one portion into a small rectangle. Keep the remaining pieces covered in cling wrap, to prevent drying out. Feed the dough through a pasta machine, starting at the thickest setting. Fold the sheet in three, to form a thick rectangle. Turn it 90 degrees and pass through the same setting 2–3 more times, until the dough becomes silky. Gradually work down the settings, dusting the dough occasionally with flour, until the desired thickness is reached. Cut the pasta sheet in half as it gets longer, to make it more manageable to work with.

**Fettuccine** Fix the appropriate attachment to your pasta machine. Trim the edges of the pasta sheets (above), lightly dust with flour and feed through the machine.

If cutting by hand, dust the pasta sheets with flour and roll up lengthways. Cut into 1½-cm (⅝-in) widths and unravel.

To dry, drape the fettuccine over a wooden rod or rolling pin for 1–2 days, until completely dry. Pasta can then be stored in an airtight container for up to two months.

If cooking the pasta fresh, put it on a tray lined with a lightly floured tea towel or twist it into bundles until required.

**Pappardelle** Trim the edges of the pasta sheets (page 46), lightly dust with flour and roll up lengthways. Cut into 2.5-cm (1-in) widths and unravel. Dry or store as described above.

**Lasagne sheets** Trim the edges of the pasta sheets (page 46) and cut out 10-cm × 12-cm (4-in × 5-in) rectangles. Lay flat on an airing rack to dry for 1–2 days, until completely dry, or (if using fresh) put them on a tray lined with a lightly floured tea towel until required.

# Fresh Egg Pasta

Serves 4 (150 g per portion)

2⅔ cups (400 g/14 oz) plain
  flour

2 teaspoons salt

4 large eggs plus 2 large egg
  yolks, lightly beaten

Combine the flour and salt in a pile on a clean kitchen surface. Make a well in the centre and pour in the egg mixture. Work the egg into the flour, stirring with a fork, until dough begins to form. Knead the dough for 10–15 minutes, until it becomes soft, smooth and elastic. If the dough seems too sticky, add a little more flour; if too dry, wet your hands and knead in some water. Shape into a ball, cover with cling wrap and refrigerate for 1 hour before rolling out.

↬ Dough can be wrapped in cling wrap and frozen for up to 3 months. Fresh pasta is best cooked and prepared on the same day.

# Fresh Spinach Pasta

Pasta verde

Serves 4 (150 g per portion)

**300 g (10 oz) spinach leaves**

**2 cups (300 g/10½ oz) plain flour**

**2 teaspoons salt**

**1 large egg plus 4 large egg yolks, lightly beaten**

Place a large saucepan of water over high heat and bring to the boil. Blanch the spinach for 10 seconds, until wilted. Drain and squeeze out as much moisture as possible. Finely chop and set aside.

Combine the flour and salt in a pile on a clean kitchen surface. Make a well in the centre, pour in the egg mixture and add the spinach. Work the egg and spinach into the flour, stirring with a fork, until dough begins to form. Knead the dough for 10–15 minutes, until it becomes soft, smooth and elastic. If the dough seems too sticky, add a little more flour; if too dry, wet your hands and knead in some water. Shape into a ball, cover with cling wrap and refrigerate for 1 hour before rolling out.

≈ Dough can be wrapped in cling wrap and frozen for up to 3 months.

# Bucatini with Spicy Tomato Sauce

Bucatini Amatriciana

Serves 4

2 tablespoons (40 ml/1½ fl oz)
olive oil

200 g (7 oz) pancetta, finely
sliced

1 medium red onion, sliced

2 cloves garlic, thinly sliced

1 long red chilli, sliced

1 tablespoon finely chopped
rosemary

¼ cup (60 ml/2 fl oz) red wine

6 large ripe tomatoes, diced

salt and freshly ground black
pepper

500 g (1 lb 2 oz) bucatini

1 cup (80 g/3 oz) grated
pecorino

Heat the oil in a large, heavy-based saucepan over low–medium heat. Add
the pancetta and cook for 5 minutes, until crisp. Decrease the heat to low,
add the onion, garlic, chilli and rosemary and sauté, stirring occasionally,
for 10 minutes, until caramelised. Add the wine and tomato and gently simmer for 15 minutes, until softened to a chunky sauce consistency. Season
with salt and pepper.

Meanwhile bring a large pot of water to the boil. Add a tablespoon of salt
and a splash of oil. Cook the pasta according to the packet directions, until
al dente. Drain and return to the pan.

Pour sauce over the pasta and toss to combine. Serve scattered with pecorino.

# Chicken & Mushroom Tortellini with Cream Sauce

Serves 4

1 quantity fresh egg pasta
  dough (page 48)

1 beaten egg, for brushing

1 cup freshly grated parmesan

FILLING

15 g (½ oz) dried porcini
  mushrooms, soaked in warm
  water for 15 minutes

300 g (10½ oz) chicken mince

1 cup finely grated parmesan

¼ cup (60 ml/2 fl oz) cream

2 large eggs, lightly beaten

1 clove garlic, crushed

2 tablespoons finely chopped
  oregano

salt and freshly ground black
  pepper

SAUCE

1 cup (250 ml/8½ fl oz) cream

150 g (5 oz) mascarpone

To make the filling, drain and finely chop the porcini mushrooms and place in a medium bowl. Add the chicken, parmesan, cream, egg, garlic and oregano and stir to combine. Season with salt and pepper. Cover with cling wrap and refrigerate until required.

To make the tortellini, divide the pasta dough into quarters. Lightly flour the bench and shape one portion into a small rectangle. Keep the remaining pieces covered in cling wrap, to prevent drying out. Feed the dough through a pasta machine, starting at the thickest setting. Fold the sheet in three, to form a thick rectangle. Turn it 90 degrees and pass through the same setting 2–3 more times, until the dough becomes silky. >

Gradually work down the settings, dusting the dough occasionally with flour, until the desired thickness is reached. Cut the pasta sheet in half as it gets longer, to make it more manageable to work with.

Bring a large pot of water to the boil. Add a tablespoon of salt and a splash of oil.

Trim each pasta sheet and cut out eight 10-cm (4-in) squares. Place a spoonful of filling in the centre of each square. Brush the edges with egg and fold the pasta over the filling to create a triangular shape and press to seal. Wrap each tortellini around your finger, crossing the two points over in the centre. Press to seal and place on a lightly floured tea towel.

To make the sauce, pour the cream into a large frying pan over medium heat. Bring to the boil and gently simmer for 3–5 minutes, or until thickened slightly. Add the mascarpone and stir to combine.

Meanwhile, in rapidly boiling water, cook the tortellini in batches for 4–5 minutes, until floating and al dente. Remove tortellini using a slotted spoon and drain over the pot. Add the tortellini to the prepared sauce and toss to coat. Serve topped with parmesan.

# Gnocchi alla Romana

Serves 4

1 L (34 fl oz) milk
1 cup (200 g/7 oz) semolina
1½ cups grated parmesan
3 large egg yolks
60 g (2 oz) butter, cubed
salt

Place the milk in a medium saucepan over low–medium heat and bring almost to boiling point. Decrease the heat to low and gradually pour in the semolina, stirring. Cook for 10–15 minutes, stirring continuously, until semolina thickens and comes away from the sides of the pan.

Remove from heat and stir in half of the parmesan, the yolks and the butter. Season with salt. Pour onto a lightly greased baking tray to about 1-cm (⅜-in) thick, cover with baking paper and refrigerate for 1 hour, or until firm.

Preheat the oven to 200°C (390°F). Grease an 18-cm × 26-cm (7-in × 10-in) ovenproof dish.

Cut rounds out of the set semolina using a 5-cm (2-in) biscuit cutter. Arrange the rounds, overlapping slightly, in greased dish. Sprinkle with the remaining parmesan and bake for 15–20 minutes, until golden-brown.

# Pumpkin, Spinach & Pine Nut Cannelloni

Serves 6–8

2 × 200-g (7 oz) packets dried cannelloni tubes

150 g (5 oz) mozzarella, thinly sliced

## FILLING

650 g (1 lb 7 oz) pumpkin, skinned, deseeded and cut into 2.5-cm (1-in) cubes

1 tablespoon (20 ml/¾ fl oz) olive oil

300 g (10½ oz) spinach leaves

600 g (1 lb 5 oz) ricotta

2 cups grated parmesan

1 cup basil, finely chopped

½ cup pine nuts, lightly toasted and coarsely chopped

3 cloves garlic, crushed

1½ teaspoons ground nutmeg

salt and freshly ground pepper

## TOMATO SAUCE

4 tablespoons (80 ml/3 fl oz) olive oil

1 large onion, finely chopped

3 cloves garlic, finely chopped

2 × 800-g (1 lb 12-oz) cans whole peeled tomatoes, coarsely chopped

½ cup (125 ml/4 fl oz) water

½ cup chopped oregano leaves

2 tablespoons tomato paste

1 tablespoon (15 g/½ oz) sugar

salt and freshly ground black pepper

Preheat the oven to 180°C (360°F). Grease a 23-cm × 33-cm (9-in × 13-in) baking dish.

Spread pumpkin on a large baking tray. Drizzle with oil and toss to coat. Bake in preheated oven for 30–40 minutes, until softened and golden-brown. Remove from the oven, mash and set aside to cool. (Leave oven on.)

To make the sauce, heat the oil in a medium, heavy-based saucepan over low–medium heat. Add the onion and garlic, and sauté until softened. Add the tomato, water, oregano, tomato paste and sugar, and stir to combine. Gently simmer for 30 minutes. Season with salt and pepper and set aside.

Place a large saucepan of water over high heat and bring to the boil. Blanch the spinach for 10 seconds, until wilted. Drain and squeeze out as much moisture as possible. Finely chop and place in a large bowl. Add the pumpkin, ricotta, parmesan, basil, pine nuts, garlic and nutmeg. Stir to combine and season with salt and pepper.

Spoon the pumpkin mix into a pastry bag fitted with a large plain nozzle. Fill the cannelloni tubes with the mix and place in a single layer in the prepared baking dish. Pour the tomato sauce over and scatter with mozzarella. Cover with aluminium foil and bake for 30 minutes. Remove the foil and bake for a further 10 minutes, until golden-brown.

# Potato, Mint & Goat's Cheese Agnolotti with Lemon Butter

Serves 4

1 quantity fresh spinach pasta
dough (page 49)

1 beaten egg, for brushing

parmesan, to serve

FILLING

300 g (10½ oz) potatoes

200 g (7 oz) soft goat's cheese,
crumbled

200 g (7 oz) ricotta cheese,
crumbled

4 tablespoons finely chopped
mint

salt and freshly ground black
pepper

LEMON BUTTER

100 g (3½ oz) butter

juice of ½ lemon

To make the filling, place the potatoes in a medium saucepan, cover with cold water and bring to the boil. Decrease the heat and simmer for 20–30 minutes, until potatoes are tender. Drain.

Peel the potatoes whilst still warm and pass through a potato ricer or mash using a potato masher. Place the potato, goat's cheese, ricotta and mint in a medium bowl and stir to combine. Season with salt and pepper. Cover with cling wrap and refrigerate until required.

To make the agnolotti, divide the pasta dough into quarters. Lightly flour the bench and shape one portion into a small rectangle. Keep the remaining pieces covered in cling wrap, to prevent drying out. >

Feed the dough through a pasta machine, starting at the thickest setting. Fold the sheet in three, to form a thick rectangle. Turn it 90 degrees and pass through the same setting 2–3 more times, until dough becomes silky. Gradually work down the settings, dusting the dough occasionally with flour, until the desired thickness is reached. Cut the pasta sheet in half as it gets longer, to make it more manageable to work with.

Trim the pasta sheets and cut out 8-cm (3-in) rounds using a fluted dough wheel. Place a spoonful of filling in the centre of each round. Brush the edges with egg and fold the pasta over the filling to create a crescent shape. Press around the filling to seal and remove any trapped air. Place onto a lightly floured tea towel.

Bring a large pot of water to the boil. Add salt and a splash of oil. Cook the agnolotti in rapidly boiling water in batches, for 4–5 minutes, until floating and al dente. Remove agnolotti using a slotted spoon, drain over the pot and transfer to serving plates or bowls.

Melt the butter in a small heavy-based frying pan over low–medium heat. When it begins to bubble, squeeze in the lemon juice. Pour sauce over the agnolotti and top with parmesan and freshly ground pepper.

# Spaghetti Vongole

Serves 4

600 g (1 lb 5 oz) fresh or 500 g (1 lb 2 oz) dried spaghetti

4 tablespoons (80 ml/3 fl oz) extra-virgin olive oil

1 medium onion, finely diced

2 cloves garlic, finely chopped

1 large red chilli, deseeded and finely chopped

½ cup (125 ml/4 fl oz) dry white wine

1 kg (2 lb 3 oz) small clams, washed (discard any shells that stay open)

½ cup chopped flat-leaf parsley

juice of ½ lemon

salt and freshly ground black pepper

Bring a large pot of water to the boil. Add a tablespoon of salt and a splash of oil. Cook the pasta for 3–4 minutes if fresh or according to the packet directions if dried, until al dente. Drain and return to the pan.

Meanwhile, heat the oil in a large, heavy-based saucepan over low–medium heat. Add the onion, garlic and chilli, and sauté until softened. Increase the heat to medium, pour in the wine and add the clams. Cover and cook, shaking occasionally, for 5 minutes, until most of the shells have opened. Discard any unopened shells. Add the parsley and lemon juice and stir to combine. Season with salt and pepper.

Transfer pasta to the pan with the clams and toss to combine.

# Penne with Sausage & Spicy Tomato Sauce

Serves 4

600 g (1 lb 5 oz) fresh or 500 g (1 lb 2 oz) dried penne

3 tablespoons (60 ml/2 fl oz) olive oil

1 medium onion, sliced

3 cloves garlic, finely chopped

4 Italian sausages, casings removed and meat crumbled

½ cup (125 ml/4 fl oz) red wine

1 × 800-g (1 lb 12-oz) can whole peeled tomatoes, chopped

2 dried red chillies, crumbled

salt and freshly ground black pepper

Bring a large pot of water to the boil. Add a tablespoon of salt and a splash of oil. Cook the pasta for 3–4 minutes if fresh or according to the packet directions if dried, until al dente. Drain and return to the pan.

Heat the oil in a medium, heavy-based saucepan over low–medium heat. Add the onion and garlic, and sauté until softened. Increase the heat to medium. Add the sausage meat, stirring to break up, and cook for 5 minutes, until browned. Pour in the wine and cook until reduced by half. Add the tomato and chilli, and bring to the boil. Decrease the heat to low and gently simmer for 15 minutes, until flavours have developed. Season with salt and pepper. Add the pasta and toss to combine.

# Beetroot & Taleggio Ravioli

Serves 4

1 quantity fresh egg pasta
dough (page 48)

1 beaten egg, for brushing

100 g (3½ oz) butter

½ cup finely grated parmesan

FILLING

2 medium beetroots (about
300 g/10½ oz each)

200 g (7 oz) ricotta cheese

½ cup almond meal

100 g (3½ oz) taleggio, finely
chopped

salt and freshly ground black
pepper

1 large egg, lightly beaten

Preheat the oven to 200°C (390°F).

To make the filling, wrap each beetroot in aluminium foil and place on baking
tray. Bake in the oven for 45–60 minutes, until tender. Set aside to cool
slightly. Peel using a small knife and chop coarsely. Place in a food processor and blend until smooth. Add the ricotta, almond meal and taleggio and
blend until combined. Season with salt and pepper. Cover with cling wrap
and refrigerate until required.

To make the ravioli, divide the pasta dough into quarters. Lightly flour the
bench and shape one portion into a small rectangle. Keep the remaining pieces covered in cling wrap, to prevent drying out. Feed the dough
through a pasta machine, starting at the thickest setting. Fold the sheet in

three, to form a thick rectangle. Turn it 90 degrees and pass through the same setting 2–3 more times, until the dough becomes silky. Gradually work down the settings, dusting the dough occasionally with flour, until the desired thickness is reached. Cut the pasta sheet in half as it gets longer, to make it more manageable to work with.

Bring a large pot of water to the boil. Add a tablespoon of salt and a splash of oil.

Trim each pasta sheet into two even lengths. On one of the pasta sheets, place spoonfuls of filling in two even rows of five. Brush egg around the filling. Place a second sheet of pasta over the top, pressing around the filling to seal and remove any trapped air. Cut out the ravioli using a fluted dough wheel. Place ravioli onto a lightly floured tea towel. Repeat the process with the remaining dough and filling.

When the water is boiling rapidly, cook the ravioli in batches for 4–5 minutes, until floating and al dente. Remove ravioli using a slotted spoon, drain over the pot and transfer to serving plates or bowls.

Melt the butter in a medium frying pan over low heat. Pour it over the ravioli and scatter with parmesan.

# Farfalle with Tuna, Capers & Rocket

Serves 4

500 g (1 lb 2 oz) farfalle

¼ cup (60 ml/2 fl oz) extra-virgin olive oil

1 small red onion, sliced

2 cloves garlic, finely chopped

finely grated zest and juice of 1 lemon

1 × 425-g (15-oz) can good-quality tuna in olive oil, drained and flaked

80 g (3 oz) wild rocket

1 tablespoon baby capers, rinsed

salt and freshly ground black pepper

Bring a large pot of water to the boil. Add a tablespoon of salt and a splash of oil. Cook the pasta according to the packet directions, until al dente. Drain and return to the pan.

Meanwhile, heat the oil in a large frying pan over low–medium heat. Add the onion, garlic and lemon zest and sauté until softened. Add lemon juice, tuna, rocket and capers and toss to combine. Season with salt and pepper.

Add tuna mix to the pasta and toss to combine.

# Lasagne Bolognese

Serves 6–8

2 × 250-g (9-oz) packets dried
lasagne sheets

1 cup grated parmesan

BOLOGNESE

2 tablespoons (40 ml/1½ fl oz)
extra-virgin olive oil

1 large onion, finely diced

2 cloves garlic, finely chopped

1 small carrot, finely diced

1 stick celery, finely diced

300 g (10½ oz) pork mince

300 g (10½ oz) veal mince

½ cup (125 ml/4 fl oz) red wine

1 × 400-g (14-oz) can diced
tomatoes

2 cups (500 ml/17 fl oz)
passata

3 tablespoons tomato paste

2 tablespoons finely chopped
oregano

3 bay leaves

1 teaspoon sugar

¼ teaspoon ground cinnamon

¼ teaspoon ground nutmeg

salt and freshly ground pepper

BÉCHAMEL SAUCE

1 L (34 fl oz) milk

1 bay leaf

2 cloves

60 g (2 oz) butter

60 g (2 oz) flour

pinch of ground nutmeg

salt and white pepper

To make the bolognese, heat the oil in a large, heavy-based saucepan over low–medium heat. Add the onion and garlic, and sauté until golden. Add the carrot and celery, and sauté for 5 minutes, or until just softened. Increase the heat to medium, add the pork and beef mince and cook for

5 minutes, stirring to break up, until browned. Pour in the wine and cook until reduced by half. Add the tomato, passata, tomato paste, oregano, bay leaves, sugar, cinnamon and nutmeg. Stir to combine and bring to the boil. Decrease the heat to low and gently simmer for 45 minutes, until thick. Season with salt and pepper.

Preheat the oven to 180°C (360°F). Lightly grease a deep 23-cm × 33-cm (9-in × 13-in) ovenproof dish.

To make the béchamel sauce, place milk, bay leaf and cloves in a saucepan and bring to boil. Remove from heat and set aside to infuse.

Melt the butter in a medium saucepan over low heat. Add the flour and cook, stirring with a wooden spoon, for 1–2 minutes. Gradually add the milk, discarding the bay leaf and cloves, and stir until smooth. Gently simmer, stirring constantly, for 5–10 minutes until thickened. Season with nutmeg, salt and white pepper. Remove from heat and cover the surface with a piece of baking paper, to prevent a skin from forming. Set aside.

Spread a thin layer of meat sauce over the base of the prepared dish and lay lasagne sheets over the top. Spread a layer of meat on top, followed by a layer of béchamel. Continue the layers, finishing with the béchamel. Sprinkle with parmesan. Bake for 35–40 minutes, until pasta is cooked and the top is golden-brown.

# Spaghetti with Prawns & Saffron Cream

Serves 4

600 g (1 lb 5 oz) fresh or 500 g (1 lb 2 oz) dried spaghetti

2 tablespoons (40 ml/1½ fl oz) extra-virgin olive oil

400 g (14 oz) raw (green) prawns, shelled, deveined and tails left on

1 clove garlic, crushed

1 dried red chilli, deseeded and finely chopped

⅓ cup (80 ml/3 fl oz) dry white wine

1 teaspoon saffron threads, soaked in ⅓ cup (80 ml/ 3 fl oz) warm water

1 cup (250 ml/8½ fl oz) cream

salt and freshly ground pepper

Bring a large pot of water to the boil. Add a tablespoon of salt and a splash of oil. Cook the pasta for 3–4 minutes if fresh or according to the packet directions if dried, until al dente. Drain and return to the pan.

Meanwhile, heat the oil in a large frying pan over low–medium heat. Add the prawns and cook for 1 minute on each side, until they change colour. Remove from the pan and set aside.

Add the garlic and chilli to the pan and sauté until softened. Pour in the wine, saffron and its liquid and cook until reduced by half. Pour in the cream and bring to the boil. Decrease the heat to low and gently simmer for 5 minutes, until thickened slightly. Return the prawns to the pan and season with salt and pepper. Add the pasta and toss to coat.

# Capelli with Sardines & Garlic Breadcrumbs

Serves 4

5 tablespoons (100 ml/3½ fl oz) extra-virgin olive oil

4 cloves garlic, finely chopped

2 cups breadcrumbs, from day-old country-style bread

500 g (1 lb 2 oz) capelli

500 g (1 lb 2 oz) fresh sardines, scaled and filleted

250 g (9 oz) cherry tomatoes, halved

4 tablespoons chopped flat-leaf parsley

2 tablespoons pine nuts, lightly toasted

salt and freshly ground black pepper

Heat 2 tablespoons of the oil in a large frying pan over medium heat. Add the garlic and breadcrumbs and fry, stirring, for 5 minutes, until crisp and golden. Transfer to a plate and set aside.

Bring a large pot of water to the boil. Add a tablespoon of salt and a splash of oil. Cook the pasta according to the packet directions, until al dente. Drain and return to the pan.

Meanwhile, heat 2 tablespoons of oil in a frying pan over low–medium heat. Cook the sardines in batches, for 1–2 minutes, until cooked. Transfer to a plate and set aside. Heat remaining oil in the pan over low–medium heat. Cook tomatoes for 2–3 minutes, until just softened. Add the sardines, parsley, pine nuts and half the breadcrumbs and toss to combine. Season with salt and pepper. Serve over the pasta, topped with remaining breadcrumbs.

# Potato Gnocchi with Napoli

Serves 4

1 cup grated parmesan, to serve

NAPOLI SAUCE

3 tablespoons (60 ml/2 fl oz)
  extra-virgin olive oil

1 medium onion, diced

1 clove garlic, sliced

1 small carrot, diced

1 stick celery, diced

2 × 400-g (14-oz) cans whole
  peeled tomatoes, coarsely
  chopped

1 teaspoon sugar

⅓ cup finely chopped basil

salt and freshly ground pepper

GNOCCHI

1 kg (2 lb 3 oz) desirée
  potatoes

1 large egg, lightly beaten

1 teaspoon salt

1¾ cups (250 g/9 oz) plain
  flour, plus extra for dusting

To make the sauce, heat the oil in a medium, heavy-based saucepan over low–medium heat. Add the onion and garlic, and sauté until softened. Add the carrot and celery, and sauté for a further 5 minutes. Add the tomatoes and sugar and bring to the boil. Decrease the heat to low and gently simmer for 45 minutes. Remove from heat and let cool slightly. Pour into a food processor and blend until puréed. Return to the pan, stir in the basil and season with salt and pepper.

Preheat the oven to 140°C (300°F). Grease a medium-sized baking dish.

To make the gnocchi, place the potatoes in a large saucepan, cover with cold water and bring to the boil. Decrease the heat and simmer for 25–30 minutes, until tender. Drain. Peel the potatoes whilst still warm and mash. Pile the potato on a clean kitchen surface and create a well in the middle. Add the egg, salt and two thirds of the flour. Mix until a dough begins to form. Add more flour as required and gently knead until just combined.

Divide the gnocchi dough into six portions and roll out into sausage lengths 1-cm (⅜-in) in diameter. Cut into 2-cm (¾-in) pieces and place on a tray lined with a lightly floured tea towel.

Reheat Napoli sauce and keep warm.

Bring a large pot of water to the boil. Add a tablespoon of salt and a splash of oil. Cook the gnocchi in batches, for 3–5 minutes, until they float to the surface. Remove gnocchi using a slotted spoon, drain over the pot and transfer to prepared dish. Place in the oven to keep warm, until the remaining gnocchi is cooked. Spoon sauce over gnocchi and top with parmesan.

❧ If not cooking immediately, gnocchi can be stored, on a tray wrapped in a clean lightly floured tea towel, at room temperature for a few hours. Do not refrigerate as gnocchi will discolour. Alternatively, gnocchi can be frozen. Lay the gnocchi on a tray and freeze until solid. Transfer to an airtight container or zip-lock bag and store in the freezer for up to one month.

# Fettuccine Carbonara

Serves 4

600 g (1 lb 5 oz) fresh or 500 g
(1 lb 2 oz) dried fettuccine

2 tablespoons (40 ml/1½ fl oz)
extra-virgin olive oil

2 tablespoons (40 g/1½ oz)
butter

200 g (7 oz) pancetta, thinly
sliced

1 clove garlic, peeled and
smashed

¼ cup (60 ml/2 fl oz) cream

4 large egg yolks

1 cup grated parmesan

salt and freshly ground black
pepper

2 tablespoons chopped flat-leaf
parsley, to serve

Bring a large pot of water to the boil. Add a tablespoon of salt and a splash
of oil. Cook the pasta for 3–4 minutes if fresh or according to the packet
directions if dried, until al dente. Drain and return to the pan.

Meanwhile, heat the oil and butter in a large frying pan over medium heat.
Add the pancetta and garlic, and cook until crisp. Discard the garlic. Pour
in the cream and simmer for 3–5 minutes, until thickened slightly. Add the
pasta to the pan and toss to coat. Remove from the heat and stir in the egg
yolks and parmesan. Season with salt and pepper.

Serve scattered with parsley.

# Fettuccine Alfredo

Serves 4

600 g (1 lb 5 oz) fresh or 500 g
  (1 lb 2 oz) dried fettuccine

100 g (3½ oz) butter

1 cup (250 ml/8½ fl oz) cream

1¼ cups (100 g/3½ oz) grated
  parmesan

2 tablespoons chopped flat-leaf
  parsley

salt and freshly ground black
  pepper

Bring a large pot of water to the boil. Add a tablespoon of salt and a splash
of oil. Cook the pasta for 3–4 minutes if fresh or according to the packet
directions if dried, until al dente. Drain and return to the pan.

Meanwhile, melt the butter in a medium frying pan over low–medium heat.
Pour in the cream and bring to the boil. Decrease the heat to low and gently
simmer for 5 minutes, or until thickened slightly. Add most of the parmesan
and all of the parsley and stir to combine. Season with salt and pepper.
Pour sauce over the pasta and toss to coat.

Serve topped with the remaining parmesan.

# Pappardelle with Creamy Walnut Sauce

Serves 4

600 g (1 lb 5 oz) fresh or 500 g (1 lb 2 oz) dried pappardelle

1 tablespoon (20 ml/¾ fl oz) extra-virgin olive oil

1 tablespoon (20 g/¾ oz) butter

1 medium onion, finely chopped

2 cloves garlic, finely chopped

2 cups walnut halves, coarsely chopped

1 cup (250 ml/8½ fl oz) cream

150 g (5 oz) mascarpone

½ cup shaved parmesan

¼ cup basil leaves, torn

salt and freshly ground black pepper

Bring a large pot of water to the boil. Add a tablespoon of salt and a splash of oil. Cook the pasta for 3–4 minutes if fresh or according to the packet directions if dried, until al dente. Drain and return to the pan.

Meanwhile, heat the oil and butter in a medium, heavy-based saucepan over low–medium heat. Add the onion and garlic, and sauté until softened. Add the walnuts and cook for 3–5 minutes, until golden-brown. Add the cream and simmer for 3–5 minutes until thickened slightly. Stir in the mascarpone, parmesan and basil. Season with salt and pepper.

Add the pasta to the sauce and toss to combine.

# Eggplant Lasagne

Serves 6–8

½ cup (125 ml/4 fl oz) olive oil

1 large onion, finely diced

2 cloves garlic, finely chopped

2 × 800-g (1 lb 12-oz) cans whole peeled tomatoes, coarsely chopped

2 tablespoons tomato paste

1 tablespoon (20 ml/¾ fl oz) brown vinegar

2 tablespoons finely chopped oregano

2 tablespoons chopped basil

1 teaspoon sugar

salt and freshly ground black pepper

4 large eggplants, trimmed and cut lengthways into 1-cm (⅜-in) thick slices

2 × 250-g (9-oz) packets dried lasagne sheets

300 g (10½ oz) provolone, grated

200 g (7 oz) buffalo mozzarella, torn

Heat 2 tablespoons of oil in a large, heavy-based saucepan over low–medium heat. Add the onion and garlic, and sauté until softened. Add the tomatoes, tomato paste, vinegar, herbs and sugar, and stir to combine. Gently simmer for 15–20 minutes, until thickened slightly and flavours have developed. Season with salt and pepper.

Preheat the oven to 180°C (360°F). Lightly grease a deep 23-cm × 33-cm (9-in × 13-in) ovenproof dish.

Place the eggplant slices and remaining oil in a large bowl and toss to coat. Heat a large frying pan over medium–high heat. Cook the eggplant slices for 1–2 minutes on each side, until golden-brown.

Spread a thin layer of sauce in the base of the prepared dish. Cover with a layer of the cooked eggplant and a sprinkling of provolone cheese, followed by a layer of sauce. Lay lasagne sheets over the top. Continue the layers, finishing with the sauce. Scatter with mozzarella and bake for 35–40 minutes, until pasta is cooked and the top is golden-brown.

# Orecchiette with Broccoli, Tomato & Ricotta

Serves 4

400 g (14 oz) broccoli, cut into florets

500 g (1 lb 2 oz) orecchiette

4 tablespoons (80 ml/3 fl oz) extra-virgin olive oil

2 cloves garlic, finely chopped

250 g (9 oz) cherry tomatoes

200 g (7 oz) ricotta, crumbled

salt and freshly ground black pepper

¼ cup grated parmesan

Bring a medium saucepan of salted water to the boil. Cook the broccoli for 3–4 minutes, until tender. Drain and set aside.

Bring a large pot of water to the boil. Add a tablespoon of salt and a splash of oil. Cook the pasta according to the packet directions, until al dente. Drain and return to the pan.

Meanwhile, heat the oil in a large frying pan over low–medium heat. Add the garlic and sauté until softened. Add the tomatoes and cook for 2 minutes, until just softened. Add the broccoli and cook for a further 1–2 minutes, until heated through. Add the ricotta and toss to combine. Season with salt and pepper. Add pasta and toss to coat. Serve topped with parmesan.

# Pappardelle with Lamb Ragu

Serves 4

3 tablespoons (60 ml/2 fl oz) extra-virgin olive oil

1 medium onion, sliced

2 cloves garlic, finely chopped

400 g (14 oz) lamb mince

½ cup (125 ml/4 fl oz) dry white wine

5 ripe tomatoes, diced

½ cup (125 ml/4 fl oz) water

¼ cup chopped flat-leaf parsley

2 bay leaves

salt and freshly ground black pepper

600 g (1 lb 5 oz) fresh or 500 g (1 lb 2 oz) dried pappardelle

1 cup grated pecorino

Heat the oil in a medium, heavy-based saucepan over low–medium heat. Add the onion and garlic, and sauté until golden. Increase the heat to medium. Add the mince, stirring to break up, and cook for 5 minutes, until browned. Pour in the wine and cook until reduced by half. Add the tomato, water, parsley and bay leaves and bring to the boil. Decrease heat to low and simmer for 45 minutes, until thick and flavours have developed. Season with salt and pepper.

Bring a large pot of water to the boil. Add a tablespoon of salt and a splash of oil. Cook the pasta for 4–5 minutes if fresh or according to the packet directions if dried, until al dente. Drain and return to the pan. Spoon ragu over the pasta to serve, and top with pecorino .

# Trenette with Potatoes, Beans & Pesto

Trenette al pesto Genovese

Serves 4

4 baby potatoes, peeled and cut into 1-cm (⅜-in) slices

125 g (4½ oz) green beans, cut in half

500 g (1 lb 2 oz) trenette

BASIL PESTO

¼ cup pine nuts, lightly toasted

1 clove garlic, roughly chopped

¼ cup parmesan, grated

¼ cup (60 ml/2 fl oz) extra-virgin olive oil

1½ cups basil leaves

salt and freshly ground black pepper

Bring a saucepan of salted water to the boil. Cook the potatoes for 2 minutes, add the beans and cook for a further 2 minutes. Drain and set aside.

Bring a large pot of water to the boil. Add a tablespoon of salt and a splash of oil. Cook the pasta according to the packet directions, until al dente. Drain, reserving 4 tablespoons of the cooking water, and return pasta to the pan.

Meanwhile, to make the pesto, place the pine nuts and garlic in a food processor and blend for 5 seconds. Add the cheese and half the oil and blend for a further 5 seconds. Add the basil leaves and the remaining oil and blend until a paste is formed. Season with salt and pepper. Transfer to a small bowl and stir in the reserved cooking water.

Add the pesto, potato and beans to the pasta and toss to coat.

# Herbed Tomato & Fontina Risotto

Serves 4

80 g (3 oz) butter

1 tablespoon (20 ml/¾ fl oz) olive oil

1 medium onion, finely diced

1 clove garlic, finely chopped

1½ cups (250 g/9 oz) arborio or other risotto rice

2 × 410-g (14½-oz) cans chopped tomatoes

2 tablespoons finely chopped sage

2 tablespoons finely chopped rosemary

1 L (34 fl oz) vegetable stock, heated

½ cup grated parmesan

100 g (3 oz) fontina, cubed

2 tablespoons finely chopped basil

salt and freshly ground black pepper

Heat half the butter and the oil in a large, heavy-based saucepan over low–medium heat. Add the onion and garlic, and sauté until softened. Add the rice, stirring to coat, and cook for 2 minutes, until translucent.

Add the tomatoes, sage and rosemary, and stir to combine. Gradually add the stock, a ladle at a time, stirring constantly. Ensure all the liquid is absorbed before the next addition. Cook for 20–25 minutes, adding the stock gradually and stirring continuously, until the rice is al dente. Stir in the parmesan and the remaining butter. Add the fontina and basil, stirring until the cheese melts. Season with salt and pepper.

# Seared Scallop & Lemon Risotto

Serves 4

3 tablespoons (60 ml/2 fl oz)
olive oil

500 g (1 lb 2 oz) scallops, roe
removed

80 g (3 oz) butter

1 medium onion, finely diced

1 clove garlic, finely chopped

1 large red chilli, deseeded and
finely chopped

finely grated zest and juice
of 3 lemons

1½ cups (250 g/9 oz) arborio
or other risotto rice

½ cup (125 ml/4 fl oz) dry
white wine

1.25 L (2 pt 10 fl oz) fish
stock, heated

4 tablespoons finely chopped
basil

salt and freshly ground black
pepper

Heat 2 tablespoons of the oil in a large frying pan over medium–high heat.
Sear the scallops for 1–2 minutes on each side, until golden-brown and just
cooked through. Transfer to a plate and set aside.

Heat half the butter and the remaining oil in a large, heavy-based saucepan
over low–medium heat. Add the onion, garlic, chilli and lemon zest, and
sauté until softened. Add the rice, stirring to coat, and cook for 2 minutes,
until translucent. >

Pour in the wine and cook, stirring, until absorbed. Gradually add the stock, a ladle at a time, stirring constantly. Ensure most of the liquid is absorbed before the next addition. Cook for 20 minutes, then add the scallops and lemon juice and cook for a further 3–5 minutes, adding any additional stock if required, until the liquid has been absorbed and rice is al dente. Stir in the basil and the remaining butter. Season with salt and pepper.

# Risotto Milanese

Serves 4

4 tablespoons (80 g/3 oz) butter

75 g (2½ oz) veal or beef marrow

1 large onion, finely chopped

1 clove garlic, finely chopped

1½ cups (250 g/9 oz) arborio or other risotto rice

½ cup (125 ml/4 fl oz) dry vermouth or white wine

1 teaspoon saffron threads, infused in 3 tablespoons (60 ml/2 fl oz) hot water

1.25 L (2 pt 10 fl oz) chicken or vegetable stock, heated

½ cup (40 g/1½ oz) grated parmesan

salt and freshly ground black pepper

3 tablespoons chopped flat-leaf parsley

Heat half the butter and the marrow in a large heavy-based saucepan over low–medium heat. Add the onion and garlic, and sauté until softened. Add the rice and cook, stirring to coat, for 2 minutes, or until translucent.

Pour in the vermouth and saffron mixture and cook, stirring, until absorbed. Gradually add the stock, a ladle at a time, stirring constantly. Ensure all the liquid is absorbed before the next addition. Cook for 20–25 minutes, adding the stock gradually and stirring continuously, until the rice is al dente.

Stir in half the parmesan and the remaining butter. Season with salt and pepper. Serve topped with remaining parmesan and fresh parsley.

# Rice with Peas

Risi e bisi

Serves 4

1 kg (2 lb 3 oz) fresh baby
 peas in their pods

1.75 L (3 pt 10 fl oz) chicken
 stock, heated

80 g (3 oz) butter

1 tablespoon (20 ml/¾ fl oz)
 olive oil

1 medium onion, finely diced

1½ cups (250 g/9 oz) arborio
 or other risotto rice

½ cup grated parmesan

2 tablespoons finely chopped
 flat-leaf parsley

1 tablespoon finely chopped
 mint

salt and freshly ground black
 pepper

Shell the peas, reserving the pods, and place in a bowl.

Remove the strings from the pods and place pods in a medium saucepan. Pour in the stock and bring to the boil. Cook the pods until tender. Drain, reserving the liquid. Place the pods in a food processor and blend until puréed.

Heat half the butter and the oil in a large, heavy-based saucepan over low–medium heat. Add the onion and sauté until softened. Add the peas and cook for 2 minutes. Add the rice, stirring to coat, and cook for a further 2 minutes, until translucent. >

Gradually add the stock, a ladle at a time, stirring constantly. Ensure almost all the liquid is absorbed before the next addition. Cook for 15 minutes, adding the stock gradually and stirring continuously. Add the purée and cook for a further 5–10 minutes, adding any remaining stock, until rice is al dente.

Stir in half the parmesan, the remaining butter and the parsley and mint. Season with salt and pepper. The mixture will be quite wet, a cross between a soup and a risotto. Serve topped with the remaining cheese.

# Gorgonzola Risotto

Serves 4

80 g (3 oz) butter

1 tablespoon (20 ml/¾ fl oz)
  olive oil

1 medium onion, finely diced

1 clove garlic, finely chopped

1½ cups (250 g/9 oz) arborio
  or other risotto rice

½ cup (125 ml/4 fl oz) dry
  white wine

1.25 L (2 pt 10 fl oz) chicken
  or vegetable stock, heated

200 g (7 oz) gorgonzola, cubed

½ cup chopped flat-leaf parsley

salt and freshly ground black
  pepper

Heat half the butter and the oil in a large, heavy-based saucepan over low–medium heat. Add the onion and garlic, and sauté until softened. Add the rice, stirring to coat, and cook for 2 minutes, until translucent.

Pour in the wine and stir until absorbed. Gradually add the stock, a ladle at a time, stirring constantly. Ensure nearly all the liquid is absorbed before the next addition. Cook for 20 minutes, adding the stock gradually and stirring continuously.

Add the gorgonzola and cook for a further 3–5 minutes, adding any additional stock if required, until the liquid has been absorbed and rice is al dente. Stir in the remaining butter and the parsley. Season with salt and pepper.

# Wild Mushroom Risotto

Serves 4

1 tablespoon dried porcini mushrooms

2 cups (500 ml/17 fl oz) warm water

3 cups (750 ml/25½ fl oz) chicken or vegetable stock

4 tablespoons (80 ml/3 fl oz) olive oil

400 g (14 oz) mixed wild mushrooms, coarsely chopped

2 tablespoons finely chopped oregano

80 g (3 oz) butter

1 medium onion, finely diced

2 cloves garlic, finely chopped

1½ cups (250 g) arborio or other risotto rice

½ cup (125 ml/4 fl oz) dry white wine

½ cup grated parmesan

salt and freshly ground black pepper

Soak the porcini mushrooms in the water for 30 minutes. Strain through a fine mesh sieve, reserving the liquid. Chop the mushrooms and set aside.

Pour the mushroom liquid and stock into a medium saucepan and bring to a simmer over medium heat. Decrease the heat to low to keep stock warm.

Heat 3 tablespoons of the oil in a large frying pan over medium–high heat. Add the wild mushrooms and oregano, and sauté until golden. Set aside.

Heat half the butter and the remaining oil in a large, heavy-based saucepan over low–medium heat. Add the onion, garlic and porcini mushrooms, and sauté until softened. Add the rice, stirring to coat, and cook for 2 minutes, until translucent.

Pour in the wine and cook, stirring, until absorbed. Gradually add the stock, a ladle at a time, stirring constantly. Ensure almost all the liquid is absorbed before the next addition. Cook for 15 minutes, adding the stock gradually and stirring continuously. Add the wild mushrooms and cook for a further 5–10 minutes, adding any additional stock if required, until the liquid has been absorbed and rice is al dente.

Stir in half the parmesan and the remaining butter. Season with salt and pepper and serve topped with the remaining cheese.

# Squid Ink Risotto

Risotto nero

Serves 4

### SQUID

800 g (1 lb 12 oz) squid with ink sacs

2 tablespoons (40 ml/1½ fl oz) olive oil

1 medium onion, finely diced

1 clove garlic, finely chopped

¾ cup (180 ml/6 fl oz) dry white wine

juice of 1 lemon

2 tablespoons finely chopped flat-leaf parsley

salt and freshly ground black pepper

### RISOTTO

80 g (3 oz) butter

1 tablespoon (20 ml/¾ fl oz) olive oil

1½ cups (250 g/9 oz) arborio or other risotto rice

¾ cup (180 ml/6 fl oz) dry white wine

1.25 L (2 pt 10 fl oz) fish stock, heated

2 ink sacs (reserved from squid)

salt and freshly ground black pepper

To clean the squid, cut off the tentacles just below the ink sac. Remove the ink sacs, place in a small bowl and set aside. Remove and discard the guts, beak and cartilage from inside the body. Peel and discard the thin, coloured membrane covering the squid and rinse under cold water. Slice the body into thin strips and the tentacles into short lengths. >

To cook the squid, heat the oil in a medium, heavy-based saucepan over low–medium heat. Add the onion and garlic, and sauté until softened. Pour in the wine and lemon juice and bring to the boil. Decrease the heat to low. Add the squid, cover, and cook, stirring occasionally, for 45–50 minutes, until tender. Stir in the parsley and season with salt and pepper.

To make the risotto, heat half the butter and the oil in a large, heavy-based saucepan over low–medium heat. Add the rice, stirring to coat, and cook for 2 minutes, until translucent. Pour in the wine and stir until absorbed. Gradually add the stock, a ladle at a time, stirring constantly. Ensure almost all the liquid is absorbed before the next addition. Cook for 15 minutes, adding the stock gradually and stirring continuously.

Add the ink, squeezing it from its sac, and cook for a further 5–10 minutes. Add additional stock if required, until the liquid has been absorbed and rice is al dente. Stir in the remaining butter and season with salt and pepper. Serve risotto topped with the squid.

෮ Store-bought squid ink can be substituted for the sacs. For this recipe use two sachets.

෮ You can ask your fishmonger to clean the squid for you.

# Asparagus & Mint Risotto

Serves 4

80 g (3 oz) butter

1 tablespoon (20 ml/¾ fl oz) olive oil

1 medium onion, finely diced

1 clove garlic, finely chopped

1½ cups (250 g/9 oz) arborio or other risotto rice

1.25 L (3 pt 3 fl oz) vegetable stock, heated

300 g (10½ oz) thin asparagus spears, trimmed and cut into 2.5-cm (1-in) pieces

½ cup grated parmesan

3 tablespoons finely chopped mint

salt and freshly ground black pepper

Heat half the butter and the oil in a large, heavy-based saucepan over low–medium heat. Add the onion and garlic, and sauté until softened. Add the rice, stirring to coat, and cook for 2 minutes, until translucent.

Gradually add the stock, a ladle at a time, stirring constantly. Ensure almost all the liquid is absorbed before the next addition. Continue for 10 minutes. Add the asparagus and cook for a further 10–15 minutes, adding the stock gradually and stirring continuously, until the rice is al dente. Stir in the parmesan, mint and remaining butter. Season with salt and pepper.

# Chicken & Spinach Risotto

Serves 4

600 g (1 lb 5 oz) spinach
leaves

80 g (3 oz) butter

1 tablespoon (20 ml/¾ fl oz)
olive oil

1 medium onion, finely diced

2 cloves garlic, finely chopped

1½ cups (250 g/9 oz) arborio
or other risotto rice

½ cup (125 ml/4 fl oz) dry
white wine

1.25 L (2 pt 10 fl oz) chicken
stock, heated

1 skinless chicken breast,
thinly sliced

½ cup grated pecorino

salt and freshly ground black
pepper

Place a large saucepan of water over high heat and bring to the boil. Blanch the spinach for 10 seconds, until wilted. Drain and squeeze out as much moisture as possible. Finely chop and set aside.

Heat half the butter and the oil in a large, heavy-based saucepan over low–medium heat. Add the onion and garlic, and sauté until softened. Add the rice, stirring to coat, and cook for 2 minutes, until translucent. Add the spinach and stir to combine.

Pour in the wine, stirring until it's absorbed. Gradually add the stock, a ladle at a time, stirring constantly. Ensure almost all the liquid is absorbed before the next addition. Cook for 15 minutes, then add the chicken. Cook for a further 5–10 minutes, adding any additional stock if required, until the liquid has been absorbed and rice is al dente.

Stir in half the pecorino and the remaining butter. Season with salt and pepper. Serve topped with the remaining cheese.

# Seafood

Italy has an extensive coastline and seafood is an important part of the cuisine. Swordfish, mussels, clams, squid and tuna can all be found on Italian menus.

When purchasing fresh fish look for full and glossy eyes – if the eyes are sunken and dull, it isn't fresh. The gills should be red and the fish should smell fresh, not fishy. Ask your fishmonger to scale and gut the fish to save on time and mess at home. Non-traditional fish varieties have been used in some recipes here due to availability and in support of sustainable fishing practices.

When using shellfish, tap any opened ones gently on the bench before cooking. If they do not close, discard.

< King Fish with Tapenade Crust (page 106)

# King Fish with Tapenade Crust

Serves 4

4 × 180-g (6½-oz) pieces king fish, or other firm white fish

## TAPENADE CRUST

¾ cup (90 g/3 oz) pitted kalamata olives, coarsely chopped

¼ cup flat-leaf parsley

1 clove garlic, coarsely chopped

½ tablespoon capers, rinsed

½ tablespoon finely chopped rosemary

2 anchovy fillets, coarsely chopped

2 teaspoons lemon juice

3 tablespoons (60 ml/2 fl oz) extra-virgin olive oil

1½ cups (1¾ oz) fresh white breadcrumbs

salt and freshly ground black pepper

Preheat the oven to 200°C (390°F). Line a baking tray with baking paper.

To make the tapenade crust, place the olives, parsley, garlic, capers, rosemary and anchovies in a food processor and pulse until coarsely blended. Add the lemon juice and gradually pour in the oil, blending to combine. Add the breadcrumbs, season with salt and pepper and stir to combine.

Place king fish on prepared tray. Press a layer of crumb mix on top of each fillet. Bake in the oven for 10 minutes, until crumbs are golden and fish is cooked through.

# Sweet & Sour Tuna

Serves 6

⅓ cup (80 ml/3 fl oz) olive oil

2 medium onions, sliced

6 × 180-g (6½-oz) tuna steaks

½ cup (125 ml/4 fl oz) red-wine vinegar

½ cup (125 ml/4 fl oz) Marsala

1 tablespoon (15 g/½ oz) sugar

¾ cup pitted green olives

¼ cup raisins, plumped in a small bowl of water for 20 minutes and drained

salt and freshly ground black pepper

Heat half the oil in a large frying pan over low–medium heat. Add the onions and sauté until softened. Transfer to a bowl and set aside.

Heat the remaining oil in the frying pan over medium heat. Cook the tuna steaks for 2 minutes on each side. Set aside with the onions. Pour the vinegar and Marsala into the pan. Add the sugar and bring to the boil, stirring to combine.

Decrease the heat to low and return the tuna and onion to the pan. Add the olives and raisins, and cook for 5–10 minutes, until sauce thickens slightly. Season with salt and pepper.

# Seafood Stew

## Cacciucco

Serves 4

4 tablespoons (80 ml/3 fl oz) olive oil

1 medium onion, finely chopped

3 cloves garlic, finely chopped

1 dried chilli, finely chopped

¾ cup (180 ml/6 fl oz) red wine

1 × 800-g (1 lb 12-oz) can diced tomatoes

1.25 L (2 pt 10 fl oz) fish stock

650 g (1 lb 7 oz) rockling, cut into 5-cm (2-in) chunks

650 g (1 lb 7 oz) John Dory, cut into 5-cm (2-in) chunks

500 g (1 lb 2 oz) black mussels, cleaned and debearded

500 g (1 lb 2 oz) clams, cleaned

1 cup chopped flat-leaf parsley

salt and freshly ground black pepper

Heat the oil in a large saucepan over low–medium heat. Add the onion, garlic and chilli, and sauté until softened. Pour in the wine and cook until reduced by half. Add the tomato and stock, and bring to the boil. Decrease the heat to low and simmer for 25–30 minutes, until slightly thickened and the flavours have developed.

Increase the heat to medium–high, add the fish, mussels and clams, cover and cook for 7–10 minutes, until mussels and clams have opened and fish is cooked through. (Discard any unopened shellfish.) Add the parsley, season with salt and pepper, and stir to combine.

# Baked Snapper in Salt Crust

Serves 4–6

2 kg (4 lb 6 oz) coarse sea salt

2 kg (4 lb 6 oz) whole snapper,
  scaled and cleaned

1 small bunch fresh thyme

salt and freshly ground black
  pepper

extra-virgin olive oil, to serve

juice of 1 lemon

Preheat the oven to 200°C (390°F). Spead a third of the sea salt over the base of a large baking tray.

Stuff the cavity of the snapper with thyme and season with salt and pepper. Place fish on prepared tray and cover completely with the remaining salt.

Bake in the oven for 45 minutes. Remove from the oven and allow to rest for 5 minutes. Crack open the salt crust and lift out the fish. Remove the skin and place fish on a serving plate. Drizzle with oil and lemon juice.

# Ocean Trout with Salmoriglio

Serves 4

4 × 180-g (6½-oz) ocean trout fillets, or other firm white fish fillets, pin boned

SALMORIGLIO

¼ cup (60 ml/2 fl oz) extra-virgin olive oil

1 clove garlic, crushed

1 teaspoon finely grated lemon zest

2 tablespoons finely chopped oregano

1 tablespoon finely chopped flat-leaf parsley

3 tablespoons (60 ml/2 fl oz) lemon juice

salt and freshly ground black pepper

Preheat the oven to 200°C (390°F). Lightly grease a large baking tray.

To make the salmoriglio, place the oil, garlic, zest, oregano, parsley and lemon juice in a large bowl and whisk well to combine. Season with salt and pepper.

Place fish on the prepared tray. Bake in the oven for 10 minutes, until fish is cooked through. Serve drizzled with salmoriglio.

# Rockling with Salsa Verde

Serves 4

4 × 180-g (6½-oz) rockling
fillets or other firm white
fish fillets

SALSA VERDE

3 cups loosely packed flat-leaf
parsley

4 cornichons, coarsely
chopped

1½ tablespoons capers, rinsed

1 clove garlic, coarsely
chopped

3 anchovy fillets, coarsely
chopped

1 tablespoon (20 ml/¾ fl oz)
lemon juice

¼ cup (60 ml/2 fl oz) extra-
virgin olive oil

salt and freshly ground black
pepper

Preheat the oven to 200°C (390°F). Line a baking tray with a large sheet of aluminium foil.

To make the salsa verde, place the parsley, cornichons, capers, garlic and anchovies in a food processor, and pulse until coarsely blended. Add the lemon juice and gradually pour in the oil, blending to combine. Season with salt and pepper. Transfer to a large bowl, add the fish and toss to coat.

Place fish on the prepared tray, drizzle with any remaining salsa and fold foil over to encase fish. Bake in the oven for 10 minutes or until fish is cooked through.

# Mussels with Tomato & Olives

Serves 4

2 tablespoons (40 ml/1½ fl oz) olive oil

8 roma tomatoes, diced

⅓ cup pitted kalamata olives

2 garlic cloves, crushed

4 sprigs dried oregano

2 bay leaves

¾ cup (180 ml/6½ oz) dry white wine

juice of 1 lemon

2 kg (4 lb 6 oz) black mussels, cleaned and debearded

Heat the oil in a large, heavy-based saucepan over medium heat. Add the tomato, olives, garlic, oregano and bay leaves and cook for 2 minutes, until tomato begins to soften.

Increase the heat to high, pour in the wine and lemon juice, and bring to the boil. Add the mussels, cover, and cook for 7–10 minutes, until shells have opened. (Discard any unopened mussels.)

# Whole Baked Baby Barramundi

Serves 4

2 × 2-kg whole barramundi

ROSEMARY OIL

4 tablespoons (80 ml/3 fl oz)
olive oil

1 small red onion, thinly sliced

4 sprigs rosemary, leaves
picked

2 cloves garlic, thinly sliced

1 teaspoon finely grated lemon
zest

salt and freshly ground black
pepper

Preheat the oven to 200°C (390°F). Line two baking trays large enough to hold the fish with aluminium foil.

To make the rosemary oil, combine olive oil, onion, rosemary, garlic and lemon zest together in a small bowl. Season with salt and pepper.

Score each fish twice in the thickest part near the head to ensure even cooking. Coat the fish and inside the cavity with the rosemary oil. Place fish on the foil and wrap to enclose completely.

Bake in the oven for 20–30 minutes, until the fish is cooked through and flesh flakes easily.

# Seafood Skewers

Spiedini di mare

Serves 4

500 g (1 lb 2 oz) swordfish, cut into 2.5-cm (1-in) chunks

16 large raw (green) prawns, peeled and deveined

16 large scallops

MARINADE

⅓ cup (80 ml/3 fl oz) olive oil

3 tablespoons (60 ml/2 fl oz) lemon juice

3 tablespoons finely chopped thyme

2 cloves garlic, crushed

salt and freshly ground black pepper

Soak eight large bamboo skewers in cold water for 1 hour, to prevent burning. Alternatively use metal skewers.

For the marinade, combine the oil, lemon juice, thyme and garlic together in a large bowl. Season with salt and pepper. Add the seafood, toss to coat, cover with cling wrap and refrigerate for 1 hour.

Preheat barbecue grill to high.

Thread two pieces of seafood onto each skewer. Cook for 2–3 minutes on each side until cooked through.

# Roasted Rockling Wrapped in Pancetta

Serves 4

4 × 180-g (6½-oz) pieces rockling, or other firm white fish fillets

salt and freshly ground black pepper

8 thin slices pancetta

3 tablespoons (60 ml/2 fl oz) olive oil

½ cup (125 ml/4 fl oz) dry white wine

½ cup (125 ml/4 fl oz) fish stock

4 parsley stalks

4 sprigs thyme

1 clove garlic, coarsely chopped

2 black peppercorns

1 bay leaf

Preheat the oven to 200°C (390°F).

Season the fish with salt and pepper. Wrap two slices of pancetta around each piece and secure with a toothpick.

Heat the oil in a large frying pan over medium–high heat. Cook the fish for 2–3 minutes on each side, seam side down first, until golden-brown. Transfer to a small baking tray. Pour the wine into the frying pan and cook until reduced by half. Add the stock, parsley stalks, thyme, garlic, peppercorns and bay leaf, and bring to the boil. Pour the liquid into the baking tray with the fish and bake in the oven for 20 minutes, until fish is cooked through.

# Mulloway with Caper & Anchovy Sauce

Serves 4

4 × 180-g (6½-oz) pieces mulloway, or other firm white fish

1 tablespoon (20 ml/¾ fl oz) olive oil

salt and freshly ground black pepper

CAPER & ANCHOVY SAUCE

½ cup (125 ml/4 fl oz) olive oil

8 anchovy fillets, finely chopped

3 tablespoons capers, finely chopped

1 tablespoon (20 ml/¾ fl oz) lemon juice

¼ cup finely chopped flat-leaf parsley

salt and freshly ground black pepper

Preheat the oven to 200°C (390°F). Line a tray with baking paper.

To make the sauce, combine the oil, anchovies, capers and lemon juice in a small saucepan over low heat. Gently warm, stirring occasionally, until the anchovies dissolve. Stir in parsley and season with salt and pepper.

Place the fish on the prepared tray, drizzle with olive oil and season with salt and pepper. Bake in the oven for 10 minutes or until fish is cooked through.

Serve drizzled with anchovy and caper sauce.

# Baked Hapuka with Fennel & Orange

Serves 4

4 small fennel bulbs with fronds attached

¼ cup kalamata olives

1 orange, segmented and zest finely grated

4 tablespoons (80 ml/3 fl oz) olive oil

4 × 180-g (6½-oz) pieces hapuka, or other firm white fish

2 sprigs rosemary

salt and freshly ground black pepper

½ cup (125 ml/4 fl oz) dry white wine

Preheat the oven to 200°C (390°F).

Cut the fronds off the fennel and set aside. Trim and discard the tough outer layers. Bring a large pot of salted water to the boil. Blanch the fennel bulbs for 10 minutes, until tender. Drain and cut each bulb into quarters lengthways.

Combine the fennel, olives, orange segments, zest and olive oil in a large bowl. Spoon half the fennel mixture over the base of a large baking dish. Place the fish, rosemary and reserved fennel fronds on top. Spoon over the remaining fennel mixture and season with salt and pepper.

Bake in the oven for 10 minutes. Add the wine and bake for a further 5 minutes, until fish is cooked through.

# Stuffed Squid

Serves 4

4 medium squid, cleaned (see page 98) with tentacles retained

1 cup breadcrumbs, made from day-old country-style bread

¼ cup chopped flat-leaf parsley

4 tablespoons grated parmesan

2 tablespoons chopped kalamata olives

3 tablespoons (60 ml/2 fl oz) olive oil

2 cloves garlic, crushed

salt and freshly ground pepper

1 small onion, finely chopped

¼ cup (60 ml/2 fl oz) dry white wine

1 × 800-g (1 lb 12-oz) can diced tomatoes

Rinse the squid under cold water, pat dry with paper towel and set aside. Cut off the tentacles and discard the tough ends. Finely chop the remaining tentacles and set aside.

Place the tentacles, breadcrumbs, parsley, parmesan and olives in a medium bowl. Add one tablespoon of the oil and half the garlic and combine. Season with salt and pepper. Stuff the squid cavities with the breadcrumb mixture and secure the ends with a toothpick. Do not over-fill as the squid will shrink a little when cooked.

Heat the remaining oil in a large frying pan over medium–high heat. Cook the squid for 1 minute on each side, until browned. Transfer to a plate and set aside. >

Decrease the heat to low–medium. Add the onion and remaining garlic to the pan, and sauté until softened. Add the wine and cook until reduced by half. Add the tomatoes and bring to the boil. Decrease the heat to low and return the squid to the pan. Cover and cook for 30–35 minutes, until tender.

Lift the squid out of the pan using a slotted spoon. Discard the toothpicks, slice each squid into three and return to the pan to coat in sauce.

# Parmesan Crumbed Flathead Tails

Serves 4

2 cups white breadcrumbs, made from day-old country-style bread

⅓ cup finely grated parmesan

2 tablespoons finely chopped flat-leaf parsley

zest of 1 lemon

½ cup (70 g/2½ oz) plain flour

salt and freshly ground black pepper

700 g (1 lb 9 oz) flathead tails, boned and skinned

2 large eggs, lightly beaten

1 cup (250 ml/8½ fl oz) vegetable oil

1 lemon, cut into wedges

Combine the breadcrumbs, parmesan, parsley, and lemon zest in a shallow bowl. Place the flour in a shallow bowl and season with salt and pepper. Crumb the flathead tails, dipping each one in flour, followed by egg and then the crumb mixture.

Preheat the oil in a large, heavy-based frying pan over medium heat. Fry the fish in batches, for 1 minute on each side, until golden. Transfer to a baking tray lined with paper towel to drain.

Season with salt and serve with lemon wedges on the side.

# Meat & Poultry

Meat and poultry are served as the *secondo piatto* or 'second plate' in a traditional Italian meal.

Meats are often cooked slowly; braised and roasted for tenderness and flavour. In dishes such as osso bucco, braised lamb shanks, and braised rabbit, the meat is cooked with herb- and wine-infused stock until it is almost falling off the bone.

If you're short on time, try the veal saltimbocca or scallopine with marsala sauce – they're quick and easy to prepare and sure to please.

< Meatballs (page 128)

# Meatballs

Polpette

Serves 4

1 large egg, lightly beaten

2 tablespoons (40 ml/1½ fl oz) milk

1 cup fresh white breadcrumbs

¼ cup finely grated parmesan

1 tablespoon finely chopped fresh oregano

1 tablespoon finely chopped fresh parsley

3 anchovy fillets, finely chopped

1 clove garlic, finely chopped

salt and freshly ground black pepper

500 g (1 lb 2 oz) beef mince

¼ cup (60 ml/2 fl oz) olive oil

Combine the egg, milk and breadcrumbs in a medium bowl and set aside to soak for 5 minutes. Then add the parmesan, oregano, parsley, anchovies and garlic. Season with salt and pepper. Add the beef and mix thoroughly. Shape tablespoonfuls into firm meatballs and place onto a tray.

Heat the oil in a large frying pan and fry the meatballs in batches for 3–4 minutes, turning, until browned all over and cooked through.

Serve with your choice of side dishes, or make a tomato sauce and serve with pasta.

# Veal Saltimbocca

Serves 4

800 g (1 lb 12 oz) veal
  scallopine

salt and freshly ground black
  pepper

8 slices prosciutto

8 sage leaves

60 g (2 oz) butter

1 tablespoon (20 ml/¾ fl oz)
  olive oil

¼ cup (30 g/1 oz) plain flour

1 cup (250 ml/8½ fl oz) dry
  white wine

Season the veal with salt and pepper. Lay a slice of prosciutto over each piece of veal, place a sage leaf on top and secure both with a toothpick. Dust the veal lightly with flour.

Heat half the butter and oil in a large frying pan over high heat. Add half the veal to the pan and cook for 2 minutes on each side, prosciutto side first, until golden-brown. Transfer to a plate and remove the toothpicks. Repeat with remaining butter, oil and veal.

Pour in the wine and boil until reduced by half. Return the veal to the pan and heat through.

❧ The name of this traditional Roman dish translates as 'to jump in the mouth'.

# Veal Scallopine with Mushroom & Marsala Sauce

Serves 4

**800 g (1 lb 12 oz) veal scallopine**

**¼ cup (30 g/1 oz) plain flour**

**salt and freshly ground black pepper**

**4 tablespoons (80 ml/3 fl oz) olive oil**

**40 g (1½ oz) butter**

**½ small onion, finely diced**

**225 g (8 oz) mushrooms, thinly sliced**

**½ cup (125 ml/4 fl oz) Marsala**

**1 cup (250 ml/8½ fl oz) cream**

Lay the scallopine between two double layers of cling wrap and beat to an even thickness using a mallet. Season the flour with salt and pepper and coat the scallopine, dusting off excess.

In a large frying pan heat the oil over medium–high heat. Cook the veal in batches, for 2 minutes on each side, until golden-brown. Transfer to a plate and set aside.

Using the same pan heat the butter over low–medium heat. Add the onion and sauté until softened. Add the mushrooms and sauté for a further 5–10 minutes, until golden-brown. Pour in the Marsala and cook until reduced by half. Add the cream and bring to the boil. Reduce the heat to low and simmer gently until thickened slightly. Return veal to the pan. Toss to coat and warm through.

# Osso Bucco

Serves 4

¼ cup (30 g/1 oz) plain flour

salt and freshly ground black pepper

4 × 300-g (10½-oz) centre-cut veal shanks

4 tablespoons (80 ml/3 fl oz) olive oil

40 g (1½ oz) butter

2 sticks celery, finely diced

1 medium onion, finely diced

1 small carrot, finely diced

2 cloves garlic, finely chopped

¾ cup (180 ml/6 fl oz) dry white wine

2 cups (500 ml/17 fl oz) beef stock

4 sprigs thyme

2 bay leaves

GREMOLATA

½ cup finely chopped flat-leaf parsley

1 tablespoon finely grated lemon zest

1 clove garlic, crushed

Preheat the oven to 180°C (360°F).

Season the flour with salt and pepper and dust the veal. Place half the oil and the butter in a large flameproof casserole dish over medium–high heat. Cook the veal for 3–4 minutes, turning until browned all over. Transfer to a plate and set aside.

Heat the remaining oil in the dish. Add the celery, onion, carrot and garlic, and sauté until golden-brown. Pour in the wine and cook until reduced by half. Add the stock, thyme and bay leaves, and bring to the boil. Return the veal to the dish, cover and cook in the oven for 1½– 2 hours, until tender. The meat will almost be falling off the bone. Remove from the oven and skim off any excess fat.

Meanwhile, to make the gremolata, combine the parsley, lemon zest and garlic in a small bowl.

Serve the osso bucco sprinkled with gremolata.

ॐ Serve with risotto Milanese (page 91) to make the traditional northern Italian dish osso bucco Milanese – a hearty winter warmer.

# Lamb with Artichokes

Serves 4

12 small artichokes

juice of 1 lemon

¼ cup (30 g/1 oz) plain flour

salt and freshly ground black pepper

8–12 lamb cutlets

¼ cup (60 ml/2 fl oz) olive oil

1 small onion, sliced

2 cloves garlic, finely chopped

100 g (3½ oz) pancetta, finely chopped

2 bay leaves

1 tablespoon finely chopped oregano

1 tablespoon finely chopped thyme

1 cup (250 ml/8½ fl oz) dry white wine

1 cup (250 ml/8½ fl oz) chicken stock

1 cup (250 ml/8½ fl oz) passata

Peel the stems of the artichokes and remove the dark, tough outer leaves, exposing the light tender ones. Trim the tops and scoop out the choke. Cut artichokes into quarters.

Fill a bowl large enough to hold the artichokes with cold water and add the lemon juice. Place artichokes in the lemon water and leave to soak for 10 minutes or until required. >

Season the flour with salt and pepper and dust the lamb. Heat 2 table-spoons of the oil in a large flameproof casserole dish or heavy-based saucepan over medium–high heat. Add half of the lamb and cook for 2 minutes on each side, until browned. Transfer to a plate and set aside. Repeat with another 2 tablespoons of oil and the remaining lamb.

Heat the remaining oil over low–medium heat and sauté the onion and garlic until softened. Add the pancetta and herbs, and cook for a further 5–10 minutes, until golden-brown. Pour in the wine and cook until reduced by half. Pour in the stock and passata, and bring to the boil. Decrease the heat to low, add the drained artichokes, cover and cook for 10 minutes. Return the lamb to the dish and cook for a further 15 minutes.

# Veal with Tuna Sauce

Vitello tonnato

Serves 6

## TUNA SAUCE

- 2 large egg yolks
- 1 tablespoon Dijon mustard
- 2 tablespoons (40 ml/1½ fl oz) lemon juice
- ¾ cup (180 ml/6 fl oz) olive oil
- 1 × 185-g (6½-oz) can tuna in oil, drained
- 2 tablespoons capers, rinsed
- 4 anchovy fillets, finely chopped
- salt and freshly ground pepper

## VEAL

- 800 g (1 lb 12 oz) veal topside
- 1 onion, roughly chopped
- 1 small carrot, chopped
- 1 stick celery, roughly chopped
- 3 parsley stalks
- 2 bay leaves
- 2 black peppercorns
- 1 tablespoon (20 ml/¾ fl oz) white-wine vinegar
- ½ tablespoon salt

To prepare the sauce, blend egg yolks, mustard and lemon juice in a food processor. Gradually add oil in a thin stream, until thickened. Add the tuna, capers and anchovies, and blend to a smooth sauce. Add a little warm water if the sauce is too thick. Season with salt and pepper.

Put all ingredients for the veal in a large, heavy-based saucepan. Add enough water to cover the veal, stir, and bring to a simmer over medium–high heat. Decrease the heat to low, cover and cook for 2–2½ hours, until tender. Leave veal in the stock to cool, then remove from liquid and slice thinly. Spoon the sauce over.

# Chicken Cacciatore

Serves 4

4 tablespoons (80 ml/3 fl oz) olive oil

1 tablespoon (20 g/¾ oz) butter

1.6 kg (3 lb 8 oz) whole chicken, cut into 8 pieces

salt and freshly ground black pepper

1 large onion, sliced

1 stick celery, finely diced

2 cloves garlic, finely chopped

½ cup (125 ml/4 fl oz) dry white wine

½ cup (125 ml/4 fl oz) chicken stock

1 × 800-g (1 lb 12-oz) can diced tomatoes

2 bay leaves

1 tablespoon chopped oregano

Heat half the oil and the butter in a large, heavy-based frying pan over medium–high heat. Season the chicken with salt and pepper, and cook in batches, for 8–10 minutes, turning occasionally until browned all over. Transfer to a plate and set aside.

Add the remaining oil to the pan and decrease the heat to low–medium. Add the onion, celery and garlic, and sauté until softened. Pour in the wine and cook until reduced by half. Add the stock, tomatoes, bay leaves and oregano, and bring to the boil. Decrease the heat to low and return the chicken to the pan. Cover and cook for 35–40 minutes, until the chicken is cooked and the sauce has thickened.

# Braised Rabbit with Fennel, Olives & Rosemary

Serves 6

⅓ cup (80 ml/3 fl oz) olive oil

¼ cup (30 g/1 oz) plain flour

salt and freshly ground pepper

2 rabbits, jointed (ask your butcher to do this for you)

40 g (1½ oz) butter

1 large onion, sliced

1 clove garlic, finely chopped

150 g (5 oz) pancetta, diced

2 fennel bulbs, trimmed and quartered lengthways

1 cup (250 ml/8½ fl oz) dry white wine

3 cups (750 ml/25½ fl oz) chicken stock

½ cup small black olives

sprig of rosemary

2 bay leaves

½ tablespoon finely grated orange zest

Preheat the oven to 180°C (360°F).

Heat the oil in a heavy-based frying pan over medium–high heat. Season flour with salt and pepper. Dust the rabbit with flour and cook in batches for 3–4 minutes, until browned. Transfer to a large casserole dish.

Heat butter in the pan over low–medium heat. Add onion and garlic, and sauté until softened. Add the pancetta and fennel, and sauté until golden. Pour in the wine and cook until reduced by half. Add stock, olives, rosemary, bay leaves and orange zest, and bring to the boil. Pour stock over the rabbit, cover and cook in the oven for 1–1½ hours, until tender.

# Pancetta Roasted Chicken

Serves 4

1.6 kg (3 lb 8 oz) whole chicken

1 small lemon, halved

4 tablespoons (80 ml/3 fl oz) olive oil

1 tablespoon chopped sage

1 tablespoon chopped rosemary

salt and ground black pepper

6 thin slices pancetta

½ cup (125 ml/4 fl oz) dry white wine

3 tablespoons (60 ml/2 fl oz)

water

Preheat the oven to 180°C (360°F).

Rinse the chicken under cold running water and pat dry with paper towel. Put the lemon halves inside the cavity and truss the legs together using kitchen string. Place the chicken, breast side up, in a roasting pan.

Combine the oil, sage and rosemary in a small bowl and season with salt and pepper. Rub the herb mixture over the chicken and wrap with pancetta, tucking the ends underneath. Pour the wine into the pan.

Cook in the oven for 1½ hours, basting occasionally, until golden-brown and juices run clear when thigh is pierced. Transfer to a serving platter, cover with foil and set aside for 10 minutes. Meanwhile, place the roasting tray over medium heat. Add the water to the pan juices and heat, stirring to combine. Pour juices over the chicken and serve.

# Rolled Roast Pork

Porchetta

Serves 6–8

2 kg (4 lb 6 oz) pork loin, boned and skinned, skin reserved

4 tablespoons (80 ml/3 fl oz) olive oil

3 teaspoons salt

4 tablespoons finely chopped rosemary

2 tablespoons finely chopped sage

2 teaspoons fennel seeds

2 cloves garlic, crushed

freshly ground black pepper

½ cup (125 ml/4 fl oz) water

⅓ cup (80 ml/3 fl oz) dry white wine

Preheat the oven to 160°C (320°F).

Score the pork skin in a crisscross pattern using a shape knife. Rub 1 tablespoon oil into the skin and sprinkle with 2 teaspoons of the salt. Set aside.

Combine 2 tablespoons of the oil, the remaining salt, the rosemary, sage, fennel seeds and garlic in a small bowl and season with pepper.

Lay the pork loin on a clean kitchen surface, trim and discard any excess fat. Turn over and spread the herb mixture over the flesh. Roll up the pork and wrap the skin around the outside. Secure firmly with kitchen string and place in a roasting pan. Pour in the water and wine, and cook in the oven for 2 hours, basting occasionally with the pan juices. >

Increase the oven temperature to 180°C (360°F).

Cook the pork for a further hour. Remove from the oven, cover with aluminium foil and set aside to rest for 10 minutes. Remove string and slice the pork into 2-cm (¾-in) thick slices. Serve drizzled with pan juices.

# Chicken Scarpariello

Serves 4

¼ cup (30 g/1 oz) plain flour

salt and freshly ground black
  pepper

8 chicken thighs

4 tablespoons (80 ml/3 fl oz)
  olive oil

60 g (2 oz) butter

1 small onion, finely chopped

2 cloves garlic, finely chopped

juice of 2 lemons

1 cup (250 ml/8½ fl oz)
  chicken stock

2 tablespoons chopped oregano

Preheat the oven to 180°C (360°F).

Season the flour with salt and pepper. Dust the chicken with flour.

Heat the oil in a large frying pan over medium–high heat. Cook the chicken
thighs for 2–3 minutes on each side, until browned all over. Transfer to a
baking tray and cook in the oven for 20–25 minutes, until cooked through.

Meanwhile, melt the butter in a medium frying pan over low–medium heat.
Add the onion and garlic, and sauté until softened. Add the lemon juice and
stock and simmer until reduced by half. Stir in the oregano.

Serve the chicken drizzled with sauce.

# Veal Sorrentino

Serves 4

1 cup breadcrumbs, made from day-old country-style bread

2 tablespoons finely chopped basil

2 tablespoons grated parmesan

¼ cup (30 g/1 oz) plain flour

salt and freshly ground black pepper

1 eggplant, cut lengthways into 8 slices

2 eggs, lightly beaten

½ cup (125 ml/4 fl oz) olive oil

800 g (1 lb 12 oz) veal scallopine

1¼ cups (310 ml/10½ fl oz) passata

8 thin slices prosciutto

8 slices mozzarella

¼ cup (60 ml/2 fl oz) dry white wine

½ cup (125 m/4 fl oz) chicken stock

Preheat the oven to 180°C (360°F).

Combine the breadcrumbs, basil and parmesan together in a medium bowl. Place the flour in a small bowl and season with salt and pepper. Pour egg into a shallow bowl. Crumb the eggplant, dipping the slices into the flour, followed by egg and then the crumb mixture.

Heat half of the oil in a large frying pan over medium–high heat. Cook the eggplant for 1 minute on each side, until golden-brown. Set aside. >

Heat the remaining oil in the pan. Season the veal with salt and pepper, and cook for 1 minute on each side until browned. Arrange the veal in a large baking dish. Top each piece with a slice of prosciutto followed by a spoonful of passata, a folded piece of eggplant and a slice of mozzarella.

Pour the wine and stock into the frying pan, bring to the boil and then pour into the baking tray with the veal. Bake in the oven for 5 minutes, until the cheese has melted.

Serve drizzled with pan juices.

# Braised Lamb Shanks with White Beans

Serves 4

¼ cup (30 g/1 oz) plain flour

salt and freshly ground pepper

4 lamb shanks

4 tablespoons (80 ml/3 fl oz) olive oil

40 g (1½ oz) butter

2 sticks celery, finely diced

1 medium onion, finely diced

1 small carrot, finely diced

2 cloves garlic, finely chopped

1 cup (250 ml/8½ fl oz) red wine

1 × 410-g (14½-oz) can diced tomatoes

2 cups (500 ml/17 fl oz) chicken stock

2 bay leaves

400 g (14 oz) dried cannellini beans, rinsed

¼ cup flat-leaf parsley

Preheat the oven to 180°C (360°F).

Season the flour with salt and pepper. Dust the lamb with flour. Heat half the oil and the butter in a large casserole dish over medium–high heat. Cook the shanks for 3–4 minutes, turning, until browned. Transfer to a plate.

Heat the remaining oil in the pan, add celery, onion, carrot and garlic, and sauté until golden-brown. Pour in the wine and cook until reduced by half. Add the tomatoes, stock and bay leaves and bring to the boil.

Return lamb to the dish, cover, and cook in the oven for 1 hour. Add the beans and cook for 30–45 minutes, until tender. Stir in the parsley.

# Beef Involtini

Serves 4

½ cup (125 ml/4 fl oz) olive oil

1 onion, finely chopped

2 cloves garlic, crushed

½ cup (125 ml/4 fl oz) red wine

2 × 400-g (14-oz) cans crushed tomatoes

1 tablespoon tomato paste

1 teaspoon sugar

4 thick (2.5-cm/1-in) slices beef fillet

¼ cup sun-dried tomatoes, finely chopped

¼ cup pine nuts, lightly toasted and finely chopped

¼ cup grated pecorino

salt and freshly ground black pepper

4 slices prosciutto, halved

16 basil leaves

Heat 2 tablespoons of the oil in a medium saucepan over low–medium heat. Add the onion and garlic, and sauté until softened. Pour in the wine and cook until reduced by half. Add the tomatoes, tomato paste and sugar, and bring to the boil. Reduce the heat and gently simmer for 20 minutes. Season with salt and pepper. Pass the sauce through a fine mesh sieve and return to the pan. Keep warm.

Butterfly the beef fillets and lay them between two double layers of cling wrap. Beat the fillets to half their thickness using a mallet, then cut in half widthways.

Combine the sun-dried tomatoes, pine nuts and pecorino in a medium bowl and season with salt and pepper.

Lay half a slice of prosciutto on each piece of beef and place two basil leaves on top. Sprinkle with the sun-dried tomato mixture. Roll up the beef to enclose the filling and secure with a toothpick.

Heat 2 tablespoons of the oil in a large, heavy-based frying pan over medium–high heat. Add half the involtini to the pan and cook for 3–4 minutes, turning, until well-browned. Transfer to a plate. Repeat with the remaining oil and involtini. Return all the rolls to the pan and pour in the sauce. Gently simmer for 25–30 minutes.

Pizza

Pizza as we know it today is thought to have evolved in Naples in the early 1800s. It was here the Margherita was later named in honour of the Queen of Italy.

In Italy, pizza bases are crisp and thin, and toppings include fresh herbs, mozzarella cheese, cured meats and rich tomato sauce.

To achieve the best results, prove pizza dough in a warm place in the kitchen without any draughts. Cold air inhibits the development of the yeast and affects the lightness of the dough.

Pizza stones, available at most kitchenware stores, create a more authentic crisp pizza base. Preheat the stone in a hot oven for at least 30 minutes. Shape the pizza base, place on top of the stone, scatter with toppings, and bake in the oven until crisp.

‹ Pizza Dough (page 156)

# Pizza Dough

Makes 4 × 25-cm (10-in) pizzas

1 tablespoon (15 g/½ oz) dry
  yeast

1 cup (250 ml/8½ fl oz)
  lukewarm water

2⅔ cups (400 g/14 oz) plain
  flour

pinch of salt

1 tablespoon (20 ml/¾ fl oz)
  olive oil

Combine the yeast and water in a small bowl. Place the flour and salt in a large bowl, and make a well in the centre. Pour the yeast mixture and oil into the well and use a fork to gradually combine the flour with the liquid. Turn the dough out onto a clean kitchen surface and knead for 10–15 minutes, until a smooth elastic ball is formed.

Place the dough in a large, lightly greased bowl. Cover with a clean tea towel and put in a warm place to prove for 1½–2 hours, until doubled in size. Turn the dough out onto the bench and knock back, punching all the air out. Divide the dough into quarters and place on a lightly oiled tray. Cover with a tea towel and put in a warm place for 20–30 minutes, until doubled in size. Dough is now ready to use.

# Capricciosa

Makes 4 × 25-cm (10-in) pizzas

1 quantity pizza dough
(page 156)

TOPPINGS

180 g (6½ oz) portobello
mushrooms, thinly sliced

8 thin slices prosciutto

180 g (6½ oz) cherry tomatoes

4 marinated artichoke hearts,
sliced

¼ cup pitted black olives

300 g (10½ oz) buffalo
mozzarella, torn

extra-virgin olive oil

Preheat the oven to 220°C (420°F). Heat two 25-cm (10-in) metal pizza trays
in the oven for 30 minutes.

Remove trays from oven and brush with oil. Stretch and shape two portions
of the dough to fit the oiled pizza trays. Allow to rest for a few minutes.

Arrange half of the topping ingredients on the bases. Drizzle with oil. Cook
pizzas for 10–12 minutes, until golden-brown. Remove pizzas from the trays
and bake on the oven rack for a further 5 minutes, until bases are crisp.
Slice and serve.

Repeat the process with the remaining dough and toppings.

# Four Seasons

Quattro stagioni

Makes 4 × 25-cm (10-in) pizzas

1 quantity pizza dough
   (page 156)

TOPPINGS

1 cup (250 ml/8½ fl oz) passata

300 g (10½ oz) buffalo
   mozzarella cheese, sliced

180 g (6½ oz) button
   mushrooms, thinly sliced

⅔ cup pitted black olives

8 marinated artichoke hearts,
   sliced

8 thin slices prosciutto

extra-virgin olive oil

Preheat the oven to 220°C (420°F). Heat two 25-cm (10-in) metal pizza trays in the oven for 30 minutes.

Remove trays from oven and brush with oil. Stretch and shape two portions of the dough to fit the oiled pizza trays. Allow to rest for a few minutes.

Spread half of the passata onto the bases and scatter with half of the mozzarella. Arrange a quarter of each topping over each pizza: one quarter with mushroom, one with olives, one artichoke and the remaining one prosciutto. Drizzle with oil and cook for 10–12 minutes, until golden-brown. Remove the pizzas from the trays and bake on the oven rack for a further 5 minutes, until bases are crisp. Slice and serve.

Repeat the process with the remaining dough and toppings.

# Spicy Salami

Makes 4 × 25-cm (10-in) pizzas

1 quantity pizza dough
(page 156)

TOPPINGS

1 cup (250 ml/8½ fl oz) passata

150 g (5 oz) thinly sliced spicy
salami, such as pepperoni or
salami sardo

¼ teaspoon chilli flakes

300 g (10½ oz) buffalo
mozzarella, torn

extra-virgin olive oil

Preheat the oven to 220°C (420°F). Heat two 25-cm (10-in) metal pizza trays
in the oven for 30 minutes.

Remove trays from the oven and brush with oil. Stretch and shape two
portions of the dough to fit the pizza trays. Allow to rest for a few minutes.

Spread half of the passata onto the bases. Scatter with half of the toppings
and drizzle with oil. Cook for 10–12 minutes, until golden-brown. Remove
the pizzas from the trays and bake on the oven rack for a further 5 minutes,
until bases are crisp. Slice and serve.

Repeat the process with the remaining dough and toppings.

# Potato & Rosemary

Makes 4 × 25-cm (10-in) pizzas

1 quantity pizza dough
(page 156)

TOPPINGS

4 medium potatoes, thinly
sliced

300 g (10½ oz) fontina cheese,
thinly sliced

1 cup (80 g/3 oz) shaved
pecorino

4 tablespoons rosemary leaves

salt and freshly ground black
pepper

extra-virgin olive oil

Preheat the oven to 220°C (420°F). Heat two 25-cm (10-in) metal pizza trays
in the oven for 30 minutes.

Remove trays from oven and brush with oil. Stretch and shape two portions
of the dough to fit pizza trays. Allow to rest for a few minutes.

Arrange half the potato slices over the bases. Sprinkle with half of each
cheese and the rosemary. Season with salt and pepper and drizzle with
oil. Cook for 10–12 minutes, until golden-brown. Remove the pizzas from
the trays and bake on the oven rack for a further 5 minutes, until bases are
crisp. Slice and serve.

Repeat the process with the remaining dough and toppings.

# Romana

Makes 4 × 25-cm (10-in) pizzas

1 quantity pizza dough
(page 156)

TOMATO SAUCE

2 tablespoons (40 ml/1½ fl oz)
olive oil

1 small onion, sliced

2 cloves garlic, finely chopped

1 × 400-g (14-oz) can whole
peeled tomatoes, coarsely
chopped

2 tablespoons finely chopped
oregano

½ teaspoon sugar

salt and freshly ground black
pepper

TOPPINGS

400 g (14 oz) buffalo
mozzarella, sliced

8 anchovy fillets

3 tablespoons chopped oregano

extra-virgin olive oil

Preheat the oven to 220°C (430°F). Heat two 25-cm (10-in) metal pizza trays
in the oven for 30 minutes.

Meanwhile, to make the sauce, heat the oil in a saucepan over medium
heat. Add the onion and garlic, and sauté until softened. Add the tomatoes,
oregano and sugar and bring to the boil. Decrease the heat to low–medium
and gently simmer for 10–12 minutes, until thickened and flavours have
developed. Season with salt and pepper, and set aside.  >

Remove trays from oven and brush with oil. Stretch and shape two portions of the dough to fit oiled trays. Allow to rest for a few minutes.

Spread half of the sauce over the pizza bases. Arrange half the mozzarella slices over the top. Scatter with half the oregano and anchovies. Drizzle with oil. Cook for 10–12 minutes, until golden-brown. Remove the pizzas from the trays and bake on the oven rack for a further 5 minutes, until bases are crisp. Slice and serve.

Repeat the process with the remaining dough and toppings.

# Four Cheeses

Quattro formaggi

Makes 4 × 25-cm (10-in) pizzas

1 quantity pizza dough
(page 156)

TOPPINGS

200 g (7 oz) fontina cheese,
grated

180 g (6½ oz) Asiago cheese,
grated

150 g (5 oz) buffalo
mozzarella, thinly sliced

125 g (4½ oz) gorgonzola,
crumbled

16 pitted black olives

extra-virgin olive oil

Preheat the oven to 220°C (420°F). Heat two 25-cm (10-in) metal pizza trays in the oven for 30 minutes.

Remove trays from oven and brush with oil. Stretch and shape two portions of the dough to fit metal trays. Allow to rest for a few minutes.

Scatter half of each cheese over the bases. Place four olives on each pizza and drizzle with oil. Cook pizzas for 10–12 minutes, until golden-brown. Remove the pizzas from the trays and bake on the oven rack for a further 5 minutes, until bases are crisp. Slice and serve.

Repeat the process with the remaining dough and toppings.

# Vegetarian

Makes 4 × 25-cm (10-in) pizzas

1 quantity pizza dough
   (page 156)

TOPPINGS

1 cup (250 ml/8½ fl oz) passata

1 medium zucchini, thinly
   sliced and grilled

1 small eggplant, thinly sliced
   and grilled

2 roasted red capsicums, sliced

¼ cup pitted black olives

4 tablespoons chopped oregano

150 g (5 oz) buffalo
   mozzarella, torn

150 g (5 oz) soft goat's cheese,
   crumbled

extra-virgin olive oil

Preheat the oven to 220°C (420°F). Heat two 25-cm (10-in) metal pizza trays in the oven for 30 minutes.

Remove trays from oven and brush with oil. Stretch and shape two portions of the dough to fit pizza trays. Allow to rest for a few minutes.

Spread half of the passata onto the bases. Arrange half of the topping ingredients on the bases. Drizzle with oil and cook for 10–12 minutes, until golden-brown. Remove the pizzas from the trays and bake on the oven rack for a further 5 minutes, until bases are crisp. Slice and serve.

Repeat the process with the remaining dough and toppings.

# Margherita

Makes 4 × 25-cm (10-in) pizzas

1 quantity pizza dough
(page 156)

TOMATO SAUCE

2 tablespoons (40 ml/1½ fl oz)
olive oil

1 small onion, sliced

2 cloves garlic, finely chopped

1 × 400-g (14-oz) can whole
peeled tomatoes, coarsely
chopped

2 tablespoons finely chopped
oregano

½ teaspoon sugar

salt and freshly ground black
pepper

TOPPINGS

400 g (14 oz) buffalo
mozzarella, sliced

½ cup fresh basil leaves, torn

extra-virgin olive oil

Preheat the oven to 220°C (420°F). Heat two 25-cm (10-in) metal pizza trays in the oven for 30 minutes.

Meanwhile, to make the sauce, heat the oil in a saucepan over medium heat. Add the onion and garlic, and sauté until softened. Add the tomatoes, oregano and sugar, and bring to the boil. Decrease the heat to low–medium and gently simmer for 10–12 minutes, until thickened and flavours have developed. Season with salt and pepper, and set aside.

Remove trays from oven and brush with oil. Stretch and shape two portions of the dough to fit pizza trays. Allow to rest for a few minutes.

Spread half of the sauce over the pizza bases. Arrange half of the mozzarella slices over the top. Scatter with half of the basil and drizzle with oil. Cook for 10–12 minutes, until golden-brown. Remove the pizzas from the trays and bake on the oven rack for a further 5 minutes, until bases are crisp. Slice and serve.

Repeat the process with the remaining dough, tomato sauce and toppings.

# White

Bianco

Makes 4 × 25-cm (10-in) pizzas

1 quantity pizza dough
(page 156)

TOPPINGS

300 g (10 oz) mascarpone
cheese

150 g (5 oz) soft goat's cheese,
sliced

½ teaspoon chilli flakes

salt and freshly ground black
pepper

90 g (3 oz) wild rocket leaves

extra-virgin olive oil

Preheat the oven to 220°C (420°F). Heat two 25-cm (10-in) metal pizza trays
in the oven for 30 minutes.

Remove trays from oven and brush with oil. Stretch and shape two portions
of the dough to fit pizza trays. Allow to rest for a few minutes.

Using half of each topping, spread bases with mascarpone and dot with
slices of goat's cheese. Sprinkle with chilli flakes and season with salt and
pepper. Cook for 10–12 minutes, until golden-brown. Remove the pizzas
from the trays and bake on the oven rack for a further 5 minutes, until bases
are crisp. Top with half of the rocket and drizzle with oil. Slice and serve.

Repeat the process with the remaining dough and toppings.

# Prosciutto & Egg

Makes 4 × 25-cm (10-in) pizzas

1 quantity pizza dough
  (page 156)

TOPPING

12 thin slices prosciutto

300 g (10 oz) buffalo
  mozzarella, torn

125 g (4 oz) cherry tomatoes

8 basil leaves, torn

extra-virgin olive oil

4 large eggs

salt and freshly ground black
  pepper

Preheat the oven to 220°C (430°F). Heat two 25-cm (10-in) metal pizza trays in the oven for 30 minutes.

Remove trays from oven and brush with oil. Stretch and shape two portions of the dough to fit pizza trays. Allow to rest for a few minutes.

Arrange half of the prosciutto, mozzarella and tomatoes on the bases. Scatter with half of the basil and drizzle with oil. Cook for 10–12 minutes, until golden-brown. Remove the pizzas from the trays, crack an egg in the centre of each and season with salt and pepper. Bake on the oven rack for a further 5 minutes, until eggs are just cooked and bases are crisp. Slice and serve.

Repeat the process with the remaining dough and toppings.

# Spicy Eggplant Calzone

Makes 4

1 quantity pizza dough
(page 156)

FILLING

4 tablespoons (80 ml/3 fl oz)
extra-virgin olive oil

2 medium eggplants, cut into
2-cm (¾-in) cubes

1 clove garlic, finely chopped

1 teaspoon chilli flakes

1 cup (250 ml/8½ fl oz) passata

½ cup pitted kalamata olives,
coarsely chopped

4 tablespoons chopped flat-leaf
parsley

salt and freshly ground black
pepper

200 g (7 oz) buffalo
mozzarella, sliced

Heat the oil in a medium saucepan over medium heat. Add the eggplant, garlic and chilli, and sauté for 5–10 minutes, until golden-brown. Add the passata and olives, and cook for a further 5 minutes. Remove from the heat, stir through the parsley and season with salt and pepper. Transfer to a bowl and refrigerate until cold.

Preheat the oven to 220°C (420°F). Heat two 25-cm (10-in) metal pizza trays in the oven for 30 minutes.

Remove trays from oven and brush with oil. Stretch and shape two portions of the dough to fit pizza trays. Allow to rest for a few minutes.

Spoon a quarter of the spiced eggplant mixture onto one half of one base. Sprinkle with a quarter of the mozzarella. Fold the dough over to encase the filling, pinching the edges to seal. Repeat with second base. Brush calzones with oil and bake for 15 minutes, until crisp and lightly golden.

Repeat the process with the remaining dough and filling.

# Bolognese Calzone

Makes 4

1 quantity pizza dough
(page 156)

FILLING

2 tablespoons (40 ml/1½ fl oz)
extra-virgin olive oil

½ small onion, diced

2 cloves garlic, finely chopped

500 g (1 lb 2 oz) beef mince

1½ cups (375 ml/12½ fl oz)
passata

1 tablespoon tomato paste

2 tablespoons finely chopped
oregano

salt and freshly ground black
pepper

100 g (3½ oz) buffalo
mozzarella, sliced

Heat the oil in a medium saucepan over low–medium heat. Add the onion and garlic, and sauté until softened. Add the mince and cook, stirring to break up, for 5 minutes, until browned. Add the passata, tomato paste and oregano, and gently simmer for 45–60 minutes, until thick and flavours have developed. Season with salt and pepper, and set aside to cool.

Preheat the oven to 220°C (420°F). Heat two 25-cm (10-in) metal pizza trays in the oven for 30 minutes.

Remove trays from oven and brush with oil. Stretch and shape two portions of the dough to fit pizza trays. Allow to rest for a few minutes. >

Spread a quarter of the bolognese sauce over half of one base and sprinkle with a quarter of the mozzarella. Fold the dough over to encase the filling, pinching the edges to seal. Repeat with second base. Brush calzones with oil and bake for 15 minutes, until crisp and golden.

Repeat the process with the remaining dough and filling.

~ Calzones are ideal for using up leftover bolognese sauce. If making fresh, the sauce can be made the night before to allow the flavours to develop and to save time on the day.

# Mushroom & Roasted Capsicum Calzone

Makes 4

1 quantity pizza dough
(page 156)

FILLING

2 tablespoons (40 ml/1½ fl oz)
extra-virgin olive oil

250 g (9 oz) button
mushrooms, thinly sliced

2 cloves garlic, finely chopped

250 g (9 oz) chargrilled
capsicum, thinly sliced

4 tablespoons chopped basil

salt and ground black pepper

250 g (9 oz) ricotta cheese,
crumbled

Heat the oil in a saucepan over low–medium heat. Add mushrooms and garlic, and sauté until golden. Remove from heat and stir in the capsicum and basil. Season with salt and pepper. Refrigerate until cold.

Preheat the oven to 220°C (420°F). Heat two 25-cm (10-in) metal pizza trays in the oven for 30 minutes.

Remove trays from oven and brush with oil. Stretch and shape two portions of the dough to fit pizza trays. Allow to rest for a few minutes.

Spoon a quarter of the mushroom mixture over half of one base. Sprinkle with a quarter of the ricotta. Fold the dough over to encase the filling, pinching the edges to seal. Repeat with second base. Brush calzones with oil and bake for 15 minutes, until crisp and golden.

Repeat the process with the remaining dough and filling.

# Cheesy Soppressa & Tomato Calzone

Makes 4

1 quantity pizza dough
(page 156)

extra-virgin olive oil, for
brushing

FILLING

1 cup (250 ml/8½ fl oz) passata

200 g (7 oz) fontina cheese,
thickly sliced

200 g (7 oz) buffalo
mozzarella, thickly sliced

12 slices hot soppressa,
coarsely chopped

12 cherry tomatoes, halved

12 basil leaves

salt and freshly ground black
pepper

Preheat the oven to 220°C (420°F). Heat two 25-cm (10-in) metal pizza trays in the oven for 30 minutes.

Remove trays from oven and brush with oil. Stretch and shape two portions of the dough to fit pizza trays. Allow to rest for a few minutes.

Spread half of the passata over the bases. Arrange a quarter of the filling ingredients over half of one base and season with salt and pepper. Fold the dough over to encase the filling, pinching the edges to seal. Repeat with second base. Brush calzones with oil and bake for 15 minutes, or until crisp and golden.

Repeat the process with the remaining dough and filling ingredients.

# Sides & Extras

A side dish of vegetables or salad, known as the *contorno*, always accompanies the second course of fish, meat or poultry. Vegetable dishes are braised, grilled, marinated and roasted, while salads are crisp and dressed with vinegar. All are flavoured with fresh herbs and drizzled with extra-virgin olive oil.

Try serving the rocket and parmesan salad alongside roasted rockling. Or roasted tomatoes and grilled zucchini with a chicken dish. For an alfresco lunch or equally satisfying evening meal serve a selection of sides (perhaps all vegetarian) with some fresh focaccia.

Extras such as tapenade, pesto and salsa verde can be made days in advance and stored in the refrigerator. Toss with some al dente pasta for a simple quick meal, or use to marinate fish, meat or poultry and then grill or bake in the oven.

< Pear, Radicchio & Walnut Salad (page 184)

# Pear, Radicchio & Walnut Salad

Serves 4

3 tablespoons (60 ml/2 fl oz)
  extra-virgin olive oil

2 tablespoons (40 ml/1½ fl oz)
  lemon juice

salt and freshly ground black
  pepper

4 heads radicchio

2 pears, quartered, cored and
  thinly sliced

⅓ cup walnut halves, lightly
  toasted

Whisk the oil and lemon juice together in a small bowl. Season with salt and pepper.

Remove and discard the outer leaves of the radicchio. Roughly tear the remaining leaves and place in a medium bowl. Add the pear and walnuts. Pour the dressing over and toss to coat.

# Rocket & Parmesan Salad

Serves 4

2 tablespoons (40 ml/1½ fl oz)
extra-virgin olive oil

2 tablespoons (40 ml/1½ fl oz)
balsamic vinegar

1 teaspoon Dijon mustard

pinch of sugar

salt and freshly ground black
pepper

125 g (4½ oz) rocket leaves

¾ cup shaved parmesan

Whisk the oil, vinegar, mustard and sugar together in a small bowl. Season with salt and pepper.

Put the rocket in a medium bowl. Pour the dressing over and toss to coat. Place in a serving bowl and sprinkle with parmesan.

# Fennel, Orange & Hazelnut Salad

Serves 4

3 oranges

2 medium fennel bulbs,
   trimmed

¼ cup hazelnuts, lightly
   toasted and coarsely chopped

2 tablespoons (40 ml/1½ fl oz)
   extra-virgin olive oil

freshly ground black pepper

Peel the oranges and cut off the pith. Slice oranges into thin rounds, removing any pips.

Thinly slice the fennel and place in a medium bowl. Add the orange slices and hazelnuts. Drizzle with oil and toss to coat.

Season with freshly ground pepper.

# Tomato & Cucumber Bread Salad

## Panzanella

Serves 4

250 g (9 oz) stale country-style bread

4 tablespoons (80 ml/3 fl oz) cold water

4 medium vine-ripened tomatoes, diced

2 small cucumbers, peeled and diced

1 small red onion, finely sliced

1 cup basil leaves, torn

1 teaspoon baby capers

4 tablespoons (80 ml/3 fl oz) extra-virgin olive oil

3 tablespoons (60 ml/2 fl oz) red wine vinegar

1 clove garlic, crushed

salt and freshly ground black pepper

Cut the crusts off the bread and discard. Tear the bread into small pieces, place in a medium bowl and drizzle with the water, to moisten.

Add the tomato, cucumber, onion, basil and capers.

Whisk the oil, vinegar and garlic in a small bowl and season with salt and pepper. Pour dressing over the salad and toss to combine. Cover with cling wrap and set aside for 20 minutes, to let the flavours develop.

# Soft Polenta

Serves 4

2 cups (500 ml/17 fl oz) water
2¼ cups (560 ml/19 fl oz) milk
125 g (4½ oz) fine polenta
1 cup grated parmesan
40 g (1½ oz) butter
salt

Place the water and milk in a large, heavy-based saucepan and bring to the boil. Decrease the heat to low–medium and gradually pour in the polenta, whisking continuously, until incorporated. Decrease the heat to low and cook, stirring with a wooden spoon, for 10–15 minutes, until smooth. Stir in the parmesan and butter. Season with salt.

# Stuffed Roasted Tomatoes

Serves 4

2 cups coarsely chopped breadcrumbs, made using day-old country-style bread

4 tablespoons (80 ml/3 fl oz) olive oil

8 medium vine-ripened tomatoes

100 g (3½ oz) provolone, diced

4 tablespoons grated pecorino

2 tablespoons chopped pitted kalamata olives

4 anchovy fillets, sliced

1 clove garlic, finely chopped

2 tablespoons chopped thyme

2 tablespoons chopped oregano

salt and freshly ground black pepper

Preheat the oven to 160°C (320°F). Place the breadcrumbs on a baking tray and drizzle with half of the oil. Bake in the oven for 10–15 minutes, until golden. Finely chop and set aside.

Increase the oven temperature to 200°C (390°F). Slice the tops off the tomatoes and discard. Scoop out the flesh and discard.

Combine the breadcrumbs, provolone, half of the pecorino, the olives, anchovies, garlic and herbs in a medium bowl. Season with salt and pepper. Stuff the tomatoes with the filling and place on a baking tray. Sprinkle with the remaining pecorino and drizzle with the remaining oil. Bake in the oven for 25–30 minutes, until tomatoes are tender but still hold their shape and stuffing is golden-brown.

# Rosemary Roast Potatoes

Serves 4

800 g (1 lb 12 oz) baby
 potatoes, washed

¼ cup (60 ml/2 fl oz) olive oil

2 sprigs rosemary

3 cloves garlic, sliced

salt and freshly ground black
 pepper

Preheat the oven to 200°C (390°F).

Place the potatoes in a large roasting pan. Add the oil, rosemary sprigs and garlic, and toss to coat. Bake in the oven for 30–35 minutes, until tender and golden-brown. Season with salt and pepper.

# Baked Artichokes

Serves 4

juice of 2 lemons

4 large globe artichokes, stalks trimmed to 2½ cm (1-in)

⅓ cup (80 ml/3 fl oz) olive oil

3 tablespoons (60 ml/2 fl oz) red-wine vinegar

2 cloves garlic, finely chopped

2 anchovy fillets, finely diced

salt and freshly ground black pepper

½ cup finely chopped parsley

Preheat the oven to 200°C (390°F). Fill a large bowl with cold water and add the lemon juice.

Prepare the artichokes one at a time to prevent discolouration. Remove and discard the dark, tough, outer leaves, exposing the light tender ones. Trim the top third of the artichoke, creating a flat surface. Scoop out the choke, open up the outside leaves and place artichoke in the lemon water. Leave to soak for 10 minutes.

Combine the oil, vinegar, garlic and anchovies in a small bowl. Season with salt and pepper. Stir in the parsley.

Place the artichokes in a deep baking dish. Pour the oil mixture over the artichokes, filling up the cavities. Cover with aluminium foil and bake in the oven for 1–1½ hours, until tender.

# Broad Beans with Mint & Salted Ricotta

Serves 4

625 g (1 lb 6 oz) young broad beans in their pods, shelled

60 g (2 oz) baby spinach leaves

¼ cup mint leaves, torn

4 tablespoons (80 ml/3 fl oz) extra-virgin olive oil

3 tablespoons (60 ml/2 fl oz) lemon juice

salt and freshly ground black pepper

80 g (3 oz) salted ricotta, shaved

Bring a large pot of water to the boil. Blanch the beans for 3 minutes, until tender. Drain and rinse under cold water, to stop the cooking process. Drain again.

Combine the beans, spinach and mint in a medium bowl.

Whisk the oil and lemon juice together in a small bowl. Season with salt and pepper. Pour dressing over the beans and toss to coat. Serve scattered with ricotta.

# Baked Fennel
# with Tomato & Olives

Serves 4

2 large fennel bulbs, trimmed

2 tablespoons (40 ml/1½ fl oz) olive oil

1 small onion, finely chopped

2 cloves garlic, finely chopped

¼ cup (60 ml/2 fl oz) dry white wine

juice of 1 lemon

2 × 400-g (14-oz) cans diced tomatoes

salt and freshly ground black pepper

⅓ cup pitted kalamata olives

2 tablespoons chopped flat-leaf parsley

Preheat the oven to 180°C (360°F).

Bring a large pot of salted water to the boil. Blanch the fennel bulbs for 10–15 minutes, until tender. Drain and cut each bulb lengthways into six. Lay in a buttered ovenproof dish.

Heat the oil in a medium, heavy-based saucepan over low–medium heat. Add the onion and garlic, and sauté until softened. Pour in the wine and lemon juice and cook until reduced by half. Add the tomatoes, season with salt and pepper, and pour over the fennel. Scatter with olives and bake in the oven for 25–30 minutes, until fennel is tender. Sprinkle with parsley.

# Marinated Grilled Zucchini

Serves 4

6 small zucchini, trimmed and sliced lengthways into 5-mm (¼-in) slices

2 tablespoons (40 ml/1½ fl oz) olive oil

MARINADE

¼ cup (60 ml/2 fl oz) extra-virgin olive oil

4 tablespoons (80 ml/3 fl oz) lemon juice

2 cloves garlic, finely chopped

2 tablespoons finely chopped mint

2 tablespoons finely chopped basil

salt and freshly ground black pepper

Preheat barbecue grill to high.

Lightly brush the zucchini slices with oil. Grill for 1 minute, turning once, until tender and golden-brown. Transfer to a medium bowl.

To make the marinade, combine the oil, lemon juice, garlic, mint and basil in a medium bowl. Season with salt and pepper. Pour over the zucchini, cover with cling wrap and set aside in a cool place to marinate for 2 hours.

# Marinated Olives

Serves 4

250 g (9 oz) black olives in brine, drained

250 g (9 oz) large green olives in brine, drained

¾ cup (180 ml/6 fl oz) extra-virgin olive oil

2 cloves garlic, finely sliced

1 tablespoon finely chopped rosemary

1 tablespoon finely chopped oregano

1 teaspoon finely grated lemon zest

½ teaspoon chilli flakes

Combine all the ingredients in a medium bowl. Cover and set aside to marinate for 4 hours.

Marinated olives can be stored in the refrigerator for up to 1 week. Bring them back to room temperature before serving as the oil will solidify in the fridge.

# Focaccia

Serves 2

1 medium potato, washed

1 cup (250 ml/8½ fl oz)
lukewarm water

1 × 7-g (¼-oz) sachet dry yeast

pinch of sugar

3 cups (450 g/1 lb) plain flour

2 tablespoons (40 ml/1½ fl oz)
extra-virgin olive oil, plus
extra for drizzling

2 tablespoons rosemary

salt

Place potato in a saucepan of cold water and bring to the boil. Decrease the heat and simmer for 20–25 minutes, until tender. Drain. Peel whilst still warm and pass through a potato ricer or mash using a potato masher.

Meanwhile combine the water, yeast and sugar together in a small bowl. Set aside in a warm place for 15 minutes to allow the yeast to develop.

Combine the potato, flour, oil and yeast mixture in a large bowl and mix until dough begins to form. Turn the dough out onto a clean kitchen surface and knead for 10 minutes, until smooth and elastic.

Place the dough in a lightly greased bowl. Cover with a clean tea towel and put in a warm place in the kitchen. Leave to prove for 1½–2 hours, until doubled in size. Turn the dough out onto the bench and knock back, punching all the air out.

Preheat the oven to 220°C (420°F). Heat a 25-cm (10-in) metal pizza tray in the oven for 30 minutes.

Remove tray from the oven and brush with oil. Stretch the dough out to a large oval shape, or two smaller ones, and place on the pizza tray. Poke indentations into the dough. Cover with a tea towel and put in a warm place for 30 minutes, until doubled in size.

Drizzle focaccia with extra-virgin olive oil and sprinkle with rosemary and salt. Bake in the oven for 25–30 minutes, until golden-brown.

# Caprese Salad

Serves 4

**4 large vine-ripened tomatoes, sliced**

**250 g (9 oz) bocconcini, sliced**

**20 basil leaves**

**4 tablespoons (80 ml/3 fl oz) extra-virgin olive oil**

**salt and freshly ground black pepper**

Arrange alternate layers of tomato, bocconcini and basil decoratively on a serving plate.

Drizzle with olive oil and season with salt and pepper.

# Green Beans with Tomato & Anchovies

Serves 4

625 g (1 lb 6 oz) green beans, trimmed

3 tablespoons (60 ml/2 fl oz) extra-virgin olive oil

4 anchovy fillets, finely chopped

3 medium vine-ripened tomatoes, diced

2 tablespoons (40 ml/1½ fl oz) lemon juice

2 tablespoons chopped flat-leaf parsley

salt and freshly ground black pepper

Bring a large pot of water to the boil. Blanch the beans for 2–3 minutes, or until just tender. Drain.

Heat the oil in a large frying pan. Add the anchovies and sauté until dissolved. Add the tomato, lemon juice and parsley, and cook until just softened. Season with salt and pepper. Add the beans to the pan and toss to coat.

# Eggplant with Tomato & Olives

## Caponata

Serves 4

2 large eggplants, cut into cubes

¼ cup salt

4 medium tomatoes

½ cup (125 ml/4 fl oz) olive oil

1 red onion, diced

3 sticks celery from the centre of the celery, diced

2 cloves garlic, sliced

100 g (3½ oz) pitted green olives

⅓ cup (80 ml/3 fl oz) red-wine vinegar

3 tablespoons baby capers, rinsed

1 tablespoon raisins

1 tablespoon (15 g/½ oz) sugar

¼ cup chopped flat-leaf parsley

salt and ground black pepper

Place the eggplant in a colander, sprinkle with salt and toss to coat. Sit the colander in a bowl and set aside to drain for 45 minutes. Rinse off the salt and pat eggplant dry with paper towel.

Meanwhile bring a medium saucepan of water to the boil. Score the tomatoes, making a cross in the base of each with a sharp knife. Blanch the tomatoes in the boiling water for 10 seconds, remove using a slotted spoon and refresh in cold water. Peel off the skin and dice the flesh.

Heat half the oil in a large, heavy-based frying pan over medium heat. Add the eggplant and fry until soft and golden-brown. Remove using a slotted spoon and drain on paper towel.

Heat the remaining oil in the pan. Add the onion, celery and garlic, and sauté until golden. Decrease the heat to low, add the tomato and cook for 10 minutes, until softened. Add the eggplant, olives, vinegar, capers, raisins and sugar, and cook for 15–20 minutes, until sauce thickens. Stir in the parsley and season with salt and pepper.

# Sweet Peppers Stewed with Tomatoes

Peperonata

Serves 4

4 tablespoons (80 ml/3 fl oz) extra-virgin olive oil

1 small onion, sliced

1 clove garlic, thinly sliced

3 large red capsicums, thickly sliced lengthways

3 large yellow capsicums, thickly sliced lengthways

2 medium tomatoes, diced

3 tablespoons (60 ml/2 fl oz) white-wine vinegar

2 tablespoons finely chopped oregano

1 teaspoon sugar

salt and freshly ground black pepper

Heat the oil in a medium, heavy-based saucepan over low–medium heat. Add the onion and garlic, and sauté until softened. Add the capsicum and cook for 10–15 minutes, until they begin to soften. Add the tomato, vinegar, oregano and sugar, and cook for a further 15 minutes, until softened and flavours have developed. Season with salt and pepper.

Serve hot or cold as an accompaniment to lamb, fish or barbecued steak.

# Braised Witlof

Serves 4

**4 heads witlof, trimmed and cored**

**¾ cup (180 ml/6 fl oz) chicken stock**

**80 g (3 oz) butter**

**100 g (3½ oz) pancetta, thinly sliced**

**freshly ground black pepper**

**1 cup breadcrumbs, made from day-old country-style bread**

**1 cup grated parmesan**

Preheat the oven to 180°C (360°F).

Cut the witlof in half lengthways and place in an ovenproof dish. Pour in the stock and dot with butter. Sprinkle with pancetta and season with pepper.

Cover with aluminium foil and bake in the oven for 15–20 minutes, until tender. Remove the foil and sprinkle with breadcrumbs and parmesan. Return to the oven and bake, uncovered, for a further 10 minutes, until golden-brown.

# Hot Anchovy Dipping Sauce

## Bagna cauda

Makes 1 cup

¾ cup (180 ml/6 fl oz) extra-
virgin olive oil

4 cloves garlic, finely chopped

10 anchovy fillets, finely
chopped

75 g (2½ oz) butter

Place ¼ cup of the oil and the garlic in a food processor and blend to form a paste.

Heat the remaining oil in a medium frying pan over low heat. Add the garlic paste and anchovies, and sauté until garlic has softened and anchovies have dissolved. Add the butter and stir until melted.

Serve warm, with raw or lightly steamed vegetables for dipping.

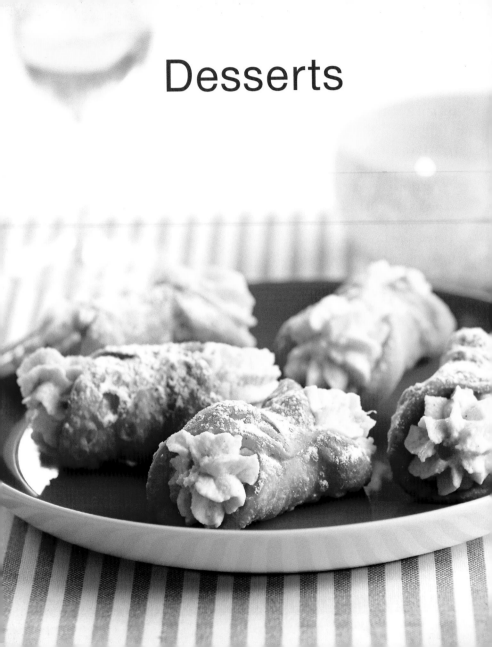

# Desserts

The final course is the *dolce* or dessert. Pastries, tarts, gelato, granita, cannoli, biscotti and tiramisu are all popular. These sweets may also be eaten as a mid-morning or afternoon pick-me-up. Flavoured with glacé fruits, chocolate, nuts, citrus, liqueurs and wine, they can be seen filling shop windows all over Italy.

Long Italian meals tend to be concluded with fresh fruit and cheese, followed perhaps by an espresso and bis-cotti. However, on festive occasions you can be sure to find an indulgent delight or two.

< Cannoli (page 214)

# Cannoli

Makes 24

oil for deep-frying

1 large egg, separated

**DOUGH**

1½ cups (225 g/8 oz) plain flour

1½ tablespoons (20 g/¾ oz) caster sugar

½ teaspoon ground cinnamon

2 tablespoons (40 g/1½ oz) butter, melted

⅓ cup (80 ml/3 fl oz) Marsala

**FILLING**

800 g (1 lb 12 oz) fresh ricotta

½ cup (75 g/2½ oz) icing sugar

1 teaspoon ground cinnamon

½ cup mixed candied peel, finely chopped

¼ cup (60 ml/2 fl oz) Marsala

To make the dough, combine the flour, sugar and cinnamon in a medium bowl. Add the butter, Marsala and egg yolk, and stir until dough begins to form. Turn out onto a clean kitchen surface and knead for 10 minutes, until smooth and elastic. Cover with cling wrap and refrigerate for 30 minutes.

Divide the dough into quarters. Lightly flour the bench and shape one portion into a small rectangle. Keep the remaining pieces covered with cling wrap, to prevent drying out. Feed the dough through the thickest setting of a pasta machine a few times. Gradually work down the settings, dusting the dough occasionally with flour, until it passes through the second thinnest setting. Cut the sheet in half as it gets longer, to make it more manageable.

Cut out rounds, using an 8-cm (3-in) round pastry cutter. Place the rounds on a lightly floured tray and cover with a clean tea towel. Roll out and cut the remaining dough.

Half-fill a large, heavy-based saucepan with oil. Heat the oil to 180°C (360°F) or until a piece of bread browns in 15 seconds when tested.

Wrap a dough disc around a lightly oiled cannoli tube. Moisten the overlapping edges with egg white to seal. Fry the cannoli, two at a time, for 2–3 minutes, turning until crisp and golden-brown. Remove using a slotted spoon and drain on paper towel. Slide shells off the tubes while still warm. Repeat the process with the remaining dough. Set shells aside to cool completely.

To make the filling, place the ricotta in a medium bowl. Sift in the icing sugar and cinnamon. Stir in the peel and Marsala until smooth. Spoon the filling into a pastry bag fitted with a large star-shaped nozzle. Fill the cooled tubes and dust with icing sugar.

&#x221D; Cannoli tubes can be purchased from specialist kitchenware stores. Unfilled cannoli can be stored in an airtight container for up to 1 month.

# Chocolate Bread & Butter Pudding

Budino nero

Serves 6

1 cup (250 ml/8½ fl oz) cream

1 cup (250 ml/8½ fl oz) milk

125 g (4½ oz) dark chocolate, coarsely chopped

4 large egg yolks

⅓ cup (70 g/2½ oz) caster sugar

½ teaspoon vanilla extract

150 g (5 oz) panettone, sliced

Preheat the oven to 180°C (360°F). Lightly grease six 180-ml (6-fl oz) capacity ramekins with butter.

Place the cream and milk in a medium saucepan over medium heat and bring almost to boiling point. Remove from heat, add the chocolate and stir until smooth. Set aside.

Whisk the egg yolks, sugar and vanilla together, until pale and thick. Gradually pour in the hot chocolate cream, stirring to combine. Arrange panettone slices in prepared ramekins. Pour chocolate cream over the top, pressing down so the bread is soaked.

Place the ramekins in a baking dish. Pour enough hot water into the dish to come half way up the sides of the ramekins. Bake in the oven for 25–30 minutes, until firm. Remove from the oven and leave puddings to cool for 20 minutes. Carefully remove ramekins from the dish. Serve warm with cream.

# Zuppa Inglese

Serves 6–8

300 g (10½ oz) store-bought plain sponge cake, cut into 1-cm (⅜-inch) thick slices

⅓ cup (80 ml/3 fl oz) rum

1 cup (250 ml/8½ fl oz) thickened cream

fresh raspberries, to decorate

½ cup flaked almonds, lightly toasted (optional)

CUSTARD

2 cups (500 ml/17 fl oz) milk

1 vanilla bean, split lengthways and seeds scraped

5 large egg yolks

½ cup (100 g/3½ oz) caster sugar

3 tablespoons (45 g/1½ oz) plain flour

RASPBERRY SAUCE

500 g (1 lb 2 oz) fresh or frozen raspberries

¼ cup (50 g/1¾ oz) sugar

2 tablespoons (40 ml/1½ fl oz) rum

To make the custard, heat the milk and vanilla bean and seeds in a medium saucepan over low–medium heat, until it almost reaches boiling point. Remove from heat.

Using an electric mixer, beat the egg yolks and sugar together until pale and creamy. Stir in the flour. Discard the vanilla bean and gradually pour the hot milk into the yolk mixture, stirring to combine. Return mixture to the pan and cook over low heat, stirring until thickened. Do not boil. ❯

Remove from heat and transfer to a bowl. Cover with a piece of baking paper to prevent a skin from forming and refrigerate until cooled.

To make the raspberry sauce, place the raspberries, sugar and rum in a medium saucepan over low–medium heat. Cook for 10 minutes, until thickened. Transfer to a food processor and blend until puréed. Pass through a fine mesh sieve.

To assemble the trifle, line the base of a 1.5 L (3 pt 3 fl oz) capacity glass bowl with a third of the sponge slices. Sprinkle with a third of the rum. Spoon over a third of the custard followed by half the raspberry purée. Repeat the layers twice more, finishing with the custard. Cover with cling wrap and refrigerate for at least 3 hours, to allow the flavours to develop.

Whip the cream in a medium bowl using an electric mixer, until soft peaks form. Spread the cream over the trifle and decorate with fresh raspberries and toasted almonds.

# Espresso Granita

Serves 4

¼ cup (50 g/1¾ oz) caster
   sugar

¼ cup (60 ml/2 fl oz) water

2 cups (500 ml/17 fl oz)
   espresso coffee

Place the water and sugar in a small saucepan and bring to the boil. Decrease the heat to low and gently simmer, stirring occasionally, until the sugar has dissolved. Pour in the espresso and stir to combine.

Pour into a shallow container and set aside to cool slightly. Freeze for 20 minutes, or until partially set. Stir with a fork to break up the ice crystals. Return to the freezer and repeat the process again.

Spoon into serving glasses and top with whipped cream.

# Orange Ricotta Fritters

Makes 24

**500 g (1 lb 2 oz) fresh ricotta
cheese**

**3 large eggs, lightly beaten**

**2 tablespoons (40 ml/1½ fl oz)
dark rum**

**1 tablespoon finely grated
orange zest**

**½ cup (75 g/2½ oz) plain flour**

**1 teaspoon baking powder**

**vegetable oil, for deep-frying**

**6 tablespoons (125 ml/4 fl oz)
honey**

**icing sugar, for dusting**

Beat the ricotta, eggs, rum and zest together in a medium bowl. Sift in the flour and baking powder and stir to combine.

Half fill a large, heavy-based saucepan with oil. Heat the oil to 180°C (360°F) or until a piece of bread browns in 15 seconds when tested. Carefully drop tablespoons of ricotta mixture into the oil and fry in batches, turning until puffed and golden-brown. Remove using a slotted spoon and drain on paper towel.

Serve immediately, drizzled with honey and dusted with icing sugar.

# Pine Nut Tart

Serves 6–8

PASTRY

150 g (5 oz) softened unsalted butter, cubed

½ cup (75 g/3 oz) icing sugar

2 large egg yolks

1⅔ cups (250 g/9 oz) plain flour

1½ tablespoons (30 ml/1 fl oz) iced water

FILLING

6 tablespoons (125 ml/4 fl oz) honey

1 tablespoon (20 ml/¾ fl oz) lemon juice

125 g (4 oz) softened butter

½ cup (100 g/3½ oz) firmly packed soft brown sugar

1 teaspoon finely grated lemon zest

½ teaspoon vanilla extract

3 large eggs

1½ cups pine nuts, lightly toasted

To make the pastry, beat butter and sugar together using an electric mixer, until pale and creamy. Beat in the eggs, one at a time, until combined. Mix in the flour and enough iced water to bring the dough together. Remove from the bowl, shape into a ball, cover with cling wrap and refrigerate for 30 minutes.

Preheat the oven to 180°C (360°F). Lightly grease a 23-cm (9-in) tart pan with removable base.

Roll out the pastry onto a lightly floured surface to 3-mm (⅛-in) thick. Press into tart pan and refrigerate for 30 minutes. >

Remove the tart case from the refrigerator, cover with baking paper and fill with pastry weights or raw rice. Bake in the oven for 20 minutes, until light golden. Set aside to cool.

Meanwhile, to make the filling, heat the honey and lemon juice together in a small saucepan over low heat, until runny. Set aside to cool. Cream the butter, sugar, lemon zest and vanilla using an electric mixer, until pale and creamy. Add the eggs, one at a time, mixing to combine. Add the honey mixture and pine nuts, and stir to combine. Spoon into the prepared tart case. Bake for 40 minutes, until set and golden-brown.

# Baked Peaches with Zabaglione

Serves 4

## PEACHES

4 ripe peaches, halved and
  pitted

¼ cup (60 ml/2 fl oz) sweet
  white wine

40 g (1½ oz) butter

## ZABAGLIONE

4 large egg yolks

¼ cup (50 g/1¾ oz) caster
  sugar

⅓ cup (80 ml/3 fl oz) Marsala

Preheat the oven to 180°C (360°F).

Place the peaches, cut side up, in an ovenproof dish. Drizzle with wine and
dot with butter. Bake in the oven for 20–30 minutes, until golden-brown.

Meanwhile, to make the zabaglione, whisk the egg yolks and sugar together
in a medium heatproof bowl, until thick and creamy. Add the Marsala.
Place bowl over a saucepan of barely simmering water and cook, whisking
continuously, until mixture has tripled in volume. Do not allow the bowl to
get too hot as this will cause the eggs to scramble.

Arrange the baked peaches on serving plates or in bowls and spoon the
zabaglione over.

# Chocolate, Ricotta & Hazelnut Ravioli

Makes 12

## DOUGH

¾ cup (125 g/4½ oz) plain flour

1 tablespoon (15 g/½ oz) caster sugar

½ teaspoon ground cinnamon

1 tablespoon butter, melted

2 tablespoons (40 ml/1½ fl oz) Marsala

1 large egg, separated

## FILLING

150 g (5 oz) fresh ricotta, drained

4 tablespoons (40 g/1½ oz) icing sugar

2 teaspoons cocoa

½ teaspoon ground cinnamon

4 tablespoons ground hazelnuts

To make the dough, combine the flour, sugar and cinnamon together in a medium bowl. Add the butter, Marsala and egg yolk, and stir until dough begins to form. Turn dough out onto a clean kitchen surface and knead for 10 minutes, until it becomes smooth and elastic. Cover with cling wrap and refrigerate for 30 minutes.

To make the filling, place the ricotta in a small bowl. Sift in the icing sugar, cocoa and cinnamon. Add the hazelnuts and stir to combine. >

Divide the dough in half. Lightly flour the bench and shape one portion into a small rectangle. Keep the remaining piece covered in cling wrap, to prevent drying out. Feed the dough through the thickest setting of a pasta machine a few times. Gradually work down the settings, dusting the dough occasionally with flour, until it passes through the second thinnest setting. Cut the sheet in half as it gets longer, to make it more manageable.

Trim each dough sheet into two even lengths. Place six evenly spaced spoonfuls of filling along one of the sheets and brush the edges of the dough with egg white. Lay the second sheet of dough over the top and press around the filling to seal and remove any trapped air. Cut the ravioli into squares using a fluted pasta cutter or sharp knife, and place onto a lightly floured tray.

Repeat the process with the remaining dough and filling.

Half-fill a large, heavy-based saucepan with oil. Heat the oil to 180°C (360°F) or until a piece of bread browns in 15 seconds when tested. Fry the ravioli in batches, for 2–3 minutes, turning, until crisp and golden-brown. Remove using a slotted spoon and drain on paper towel.

Dust with icing sugar and serve immediately.

# Tiramisu

Serves 8

4 large eggs, separated

½ cup (100 g/3½ oz) caster sugar

500 g (1 lb 2 oz) mascarpone

⅓ cup (80 ml/3 fl oz) brandy

¾ cup (180 ml/6 fl oz) espresso coffee

20 savoiardi (Italian sponge finger biscuits)

dutch cocoa, for dusting

Beat the egg yolks and sugar together in a medium bowl until thick and pale. Add the mascarpone and 2 tablespoons of the brandy and stir to combine.

Using an electric mixer, whip the egg whites until soft peaks form. Stir one third of the whites into the mascarpone mixture, then gently fold in the remainder.

Combine the coffee and remaining brandy in a small bowl. Dip half the biscuits, one at a time, in the coffee to moisten. Arrange in a single layer in a deep 20-cm (8-in) square dish. Spread with half the mascarpone mixture and dust with cocoa. Repeat layers. Cover with cling wrap and refrigerate for at least 4 hours.

To serve, dust generously with cocoa.

# Amaretti Baked Apples

Serves 4

4 tart cooking apples, such as Granny Smith

crème fraîche or mascarpone, to serve (optional)

SYRUP

1½ cups (375 ml/12½ fl oz) apple juice

2 tablespoons (40 ml/1½ fl oz) honey

FILLING

4 amaretti biscuits, crushed

2 tablespoons ground walnuts

2 tablespoons ground almonds

1 tablespoon soft brown sugar

1 tablespoon softened butter

1 teaspoon lemon zest

½ teaspoon ground cinnamon

Preheat the oven to 180°C (360°F).

Heat the apple juice and honey together in a small saucepan over low heat, until the honey melts. Set aside.

To make the filling, combine the biscuits, walnuts, ground almonds, sugar, butter, lemon zest and cinnamon together in a small bowl.

Core the apples and score the skin around the circumference, so that it splits neatly during cooking. Stuff the apples with amaretti filling and arrange upright in a small baking dish. Pour the syrup around the apples and bake, uncovered, for 35–45 minutes, until tender. Serve drizzled with syrup, with crème fraîche or mascarpone if desired.

# Vanilla Panna Cotta

Serves 4

sweet almond oil or
  unflavoured oil, to grease

2 cups (500 ml/17 fl oz) double
  cream

½ cup (100 g/3½ oz) caster
  sugar

2 vanilla beans, split
  lengthways and seeds
  scraped

2 gelatine leaves

berries, to serve

Lightly grease four 125-ml (4-fl oz) capacity ramekins with sweet almond or unflavoured oil.

Combine the cream, sugar and vanilla bean and seeds in a medium saucepan and bring almost to boiling point. Decrease the heat and gently simmer for 5 minutes.

Soak the gelatine leaves in a small bowl of cold water, until softened. Squeeze out the water and stir leaves into the cream mixture. Strain cream through a fine mesh sieve into a jug. Set aside to cool slightly.

Pour the cream into the prepared moulds and refrigerate for 6 hours, or until set. To turn out, run a small knife around the edge of each panna cotta to loosen, and invert onto a serving plate.

Serve with seasonal berries.

# Walnut Tart

Torta di noci

Serves 8–10

1 egg yolk, for glazing

icing sugar, for dusting

PASTRY

225 g (8 oz) softened butter

3 cups (450 g/1 lb) plain flour

1 cup (200 g/7 oz) caster sugar

1 teaspoon ground cinnamon

3 large egg yolks

2 teaspoons lemon zest

FILLING

200 g (7 oz) walnut halves

3 × 1-cm (⅜-in) thick slices sourdough bread, crusts removed and coarsely chopped

6 tablespoons (125 ml/4 fl oz) honey

2 tablespoons (40 ml/1½ fl oz) dark rum

To make the pastry, rub the butter into the flour in a medium bowl, until mixture resembles coarse breadcrumbs. Stir in the sugar and cinnamon. Add the egg yolks and zest, and mix until dough begins to form. Shape the dough into a disc, cover with cling wrap and refrigerate for 30 minutes.

Preheat the oven to 190°C (375°F). Lightly grease a 20-cm (8-in) tart pan with a removable base.

To make the filling, place the walnuts and bread into a food processor and pulse to make coarse crumbs. Transfer to a medium bowl.

Heat the honey and rum in a small saucepan until runny. Pour over the walnut mixture and stir to combine. Set aside to cool.

Divide the pastry into two pieces. Roll out one portion between two pieces of lightly greased baking paper and fit into the prepared pan, leaving the edges hanging over a little. Sprinkle the filling over the top.

Roll out the remaining piece of dough in the same way and lay it over the filling. Pinch the edges together to seal, and trim off any excess dough. Make a few holes in the top, for steam to escape, and brush with egg yolk.

Bake in the oven for 30–35 minutes, until golden-brown. Allow to cool in the pan for 10 minutes. Remove tart from the pan and place on a wire rack to cool completely. Dust heavily with icing sugar.

# Limoncello & Mascarpone Gelato

Serves 4–6

½ cup (125 ml/4 fl oz) freshly
squeezed lemon juice

½ cup (125 ml/4 fl oz) milk

6 large egg yolks

1 cup (200 g/7 oz) caster sugar

1 teaspoon lemon zest

½ cup (125 ml/4 fl oz)
limoncello liqueur

500 g (1 lb 2 oz) mascarpone

Place the lemon juice in a small saucepan over medium–high heat and simmer until reduced by half. Set aside to cool.

Heat the milk in a medium saucepan over low–medium heat, until it almost reaches boiling point. Remove from the heat.

Beat the egg yolks, sugar and lemon zest together in a medium bowl, until pale and thick. Gradually pour the hot milk into the yolk mixture, stirring to combine. Return mixture to the pan and cook over low heat, stirring, until slightly thickened. Do not boil. Remove from the heat, transfer to a bowl and refrigerate until cooled.

Add the reduced lemon juice and limoncello to the yolk mixture. Stir through the mascarpone. Pour into an ice-cream machine and churn, according to manufacturer's instructions, until frozen. Transfer to a freezer proof container and freeze for 3 hours, or until required.

# Torrone Semifreddo

Serves 12

almond oil, for greasing
½ cup (125 ml/4 fl oz) milk
6 large egg yolks
1 cup (200 g/7 oz) caster sugar
1 teaspoon vanilla extract

1 tablespoon (20 ml/¾ fl oz) lemon juice
1 teaspoon lemon zest
3 cups (750 ml/25 fl oz) cream
200 g (7 oz) torrone, chopped

Line a 10-cm × 21-cm (4-in × 8½-in) loaf tin with aluminium foil, followed by a double layer of cling wrap (leaving a 10-cm/4-in overhang on both sides). Lightly grease with almond oil.

Place the milk in a small saucepan over medium heat and bring to the boil.

Beat the egg yolks, sugar and vanilla until pale and thick. Gradually pour in the hot milk and beat for 5–8 minutes, until cooled. Stir in the lemon juice and zest. Cover with cling wrap and refrigerate until chilled.

In a separate bowl whip the cream until soft peaks form. Fold cream and torrone into the chilled egg mixture. Pour into prepared tin and fold cling wrap over to cover. Freeze for 4–6 hours, until frozen but not too hard.

↝ Torrone, Italian nougat, can be purchased from Italian grocers. Substitute with conventional nougat if unable to find.

# Orange & Fig Ricotta Cake

Serves 10–12

zest and juice of 2 oranges

1½ cups finely chopped dried
    figs

625 g (1 lb 6 oz) firm ricotta

3 whole large eggs, plus
    9 large eggs, separated

¾ cup candied peel

1 cup (200 g/7 oz) caster sugar

1 cup (150 g/5 oz) plain flour

½ cup flaked almonds

Preheat the oven to 180°C (360°F). Lightly grease a 25-cm (10-in) round springform cake pan and line the base with baking paper.

Heat the orange juice and zest in a small saucepan over low–medium heat. Add the figs and set aside to soak for 20 minutes.

Whisk the ricotta, whole eggs, egg yolks, peel, sugar and flour in a large bowl, until combined. Stir in the soaked figs and juice.

Whisk the egg whites in a medium bowl until stiff peaks form. Fold one third of the whites through the fig mixture and then fold through the remainder. Pour into the prepared pan and sprinkle with flaked almonds. Bake in the oven for 60 minutes, until the centre is firm to touch and a skewer comes out clean when tested. Leave the cake to cool in the pan for 10 minutes before turning out onto a rack to cool completely.

# Pistachio & Almond Biscotti

Makes about 50 biscuits

¾ cup (150 g/5 oz) caster
  sugar

2 large eggs

1 teaspoon vanilla extract

1 teaspoon orange zest

2 cups (300 g/10½ oz) plain
  flour

1 teaspoon baking powder

⅓ cup pistachios

⅓ cup whole almonds

Preheat the oven to 180°C (360°F). Line two trays with baking paper.

Beat the sugar, eggs, vanilla and orange zest together, until thick and pale. Sift in the flour and baking powder. Add the nuts and stir to combine. Turn the mixture out onto a lightly floured surface. Divide the dough in half and shape into logs approximately 25-cm (10-in) long.

Place logs onto the prepared trays and flatten slightly. Bake in the oven for 20–25 minutes, until firm. Remove from the oven and set aside to cool.

Decrease oven temperature to 140°C (275°F). Cut the loaves into thick slices. Place on trays and bake in the oven for 15 minutes, until golden and crisp. Transfer onto a wire rack to cool completely.

ॐ Store biscotti in an airtight container for up to 1 month.

# Special Ingredients

**AGNOLOTTI** Semi-circular pockets of pasta stuffed with a mix of cheese and meats, or puréed vegetables. The name means 'lambs ears'.

**ARANCINI** Cold risotto rolled in bread crumbs and fried until golden-brown and warmed through.

**ARBORIO** A short-grain rice used to make risotto. Other varieties used for risotto are carnaroli and vialone.

**BRESAOLA** Air-dried salted beef. Substitute with prosciutto if unable to find.

**BUCATINI** Thick spaghetti-shaped tubular pasta.

**CANNELLONI** Large tubes of pasta, suitable for stuffing.

**CAVOLO NERO** A long-leafed variety of winter cabbage. Substitute with cabbage or curly kale if unable to find.

**CORNICHONS** Little pickled cucumbers.

**CRÈME FRAÎCHE** A type of soured cream that is thicker and milder in flavour than regular sour cream.

**CROSTINI** Thin slices of bread that are either lightly browned under the grill or fried in butter or oil.

**FARFALLE** Pasta resembling bow ties or butterflies.

**FETTUCINE** Long flat ribbons of pasta.

**FONTINA CHEESE** An Italian cheese made from cow's milk, suited to melting.

**FUSILLI** Pasta spirals.

**GNOCCHI** Small dumplings made from a dough of mashed potato or flour.

**GORGONZOLA** A creamy blue cheese made from cow's milk.

**GRANA PADANO** A mild parmesan that has been aged for six months; *see also* Parmigiano-Reggiano.

**LIMONCELLO** An Italian spirit infused with lemon zest.

**MASCARPONE** A thick creamy cheese made from fresh cream.

**ORECCHIETTE** Pasta shaped like small bowls – the name means 'little ears' in Italian.

**PANCETTA** A dry-cured meat that has been salted and spiced. Made from the pork belly, it can be 'rolled' or 'flat'.

**PANETTONE** Italian yeast cake made with dried fruit and candied peel.

**PAPPARDELLE** Long flat wide ribbons of pasta.

**PARMESAN** Sharp-flavoured cheese made from cow's milk; *see also* Parmigiano-Reggiano.

**PARMIGIANO-REGGIANO** A hard, sharp-flavoured cheese made from cow's milk and aged for at least fourteen months. The white matrix insignia covering the rind is what separates it from other grana or parmesans. Well-known varieties are *grana padano* (a milder cheese aged for six months that is particularly good for grating) and *pecorino* (sold fresh or aged, also good for grating).

**PASSATA** A sauce made from fresh tomatoes that have been put through a food mill.

**PECORINO** A variety of parmesan. *See also* Parmigiano-Reggiano.

**POLENTA** Flavoured with stock or butter during the cooking stage, polenta (also known as cornmeal) can be soft, baked or grilled, and is usually served as a side dish.

**PROSCIUTTO** An Italian ham that has been salted and then air-dried for up to two years.

**PROVOLONE** A semi-hard Italian cheese. There are numerous varieties, with flavours ranging from sharp and strong to sweet and mild.

**RISONI** Small, grain-shaped pasta, similar in appearance to grains of rice.

**SQUID INK** The black ink of the squid, it is mild in flavour and can be used to colour pasta or rice.

**WITLOF** Related to the endive, this leafy green has a slightly bitter taste.

# Conversions

*(Note: all conversions are approximate)*

Important note: All cup and spoon measures given in this book are based on Australian standards. The most important thing to remember is that an Australian cup = 250 ml, while an American cup = 237 ml and a British cup = 284 ml. Also, an Australian tablespoon is equivalent to 4 teaspoons, not 3 teaspoons as in the United States and Britain. US equivalents have been provided throughout for all liquid cup/spoon measures. Equivalents for dry ingredients measured in cups/spoons have been included for flour, sugar and rising agents such as baking powder. For other dry ingredients (chopped vegetables, nuts, etc.), American cooks should be generous with their cup measures – slight variations in quantities of such ingredients are unlikely to affect results.

## VOLUME

| Australian cups/spoons | Millilitres | US fluid ounces |
|---|---|---|
| *1 teaspoon | 5 ml | |
| 1 tablespoon (4 teaspoons) | 20 ml | ¾ fl oz |
| 1½ tablespoons | 30 ml | 1 fl oz |
| 2 tablespoons | 40 ml | 1½ fl oz |
| ¼ cup | 60 ml | 2 fl oz |
| ⅓ cup | 80 ml | 3 fl oz |
| ½ cup | 125 ml | 4 fl oz |
| ¾ cup | 180 ml | 6 fl oz |
| 1 cup | 250 ml | 8½ fl oz |
| 4 cups | 1 L | 34 fl oz |

*the volume of a teaspoon is the same around the world

## SIZE

| Centimetres | Inches |
|---|---|
| 1 cm | ³⁄₈ in |
| 2 cm | ³⁄₄ in |
| 2.5 cm | 1 in |
| 5 cm | 2 in |
| 10 cm | 4 in |
| 15 cm | 6 in |
| 20 cm | 8 in |
| 30 cm | 12 in |

## TEMPERATURE

| Celsius | Fahrenheit |
|---|---|
| 150°C | 300°F |
| 160°C | 320°F |
| 170°C | 340°F |
| 180°C | 360°F |
| 190°C | 375°F |
| 200°C | 390°F |
| 210°C | 410°F |
| 220°C | 420°F |

## WEIGHT

| Grams | Ounces |
|---|---|
| 15 g | ½ oz |
| 30 g | 1 oz |
| 60 g | 2 oz |
| 85 g | 3 oz |
| 110 g | 4 oz |
| 140 g | 5 oz |
| 170 g | 6 oz |
| 200 g | 7 oz |
| 225 g | 8 oz (½ lb) |
| 450 g | 16 oz (1 lb) |
| 500 g | 1 lb 2 oz |
| 900 g | 2 lb |
| 1 kg | 2 lb 3 oz |

# Index

LONDON, NEW YORK, MUNICH,
MELBOURNE and DELHI

First published in Great Britain in 2011 by
Dorling Kindersley, 80 Strand, London, WC2R 0RL

A Penguin Company

Published by Penguin Group (Australia), 2010
250 Camberwell Road, Camberwell, Victoria 3124, Australia
(a division of Pearson Australia Group Pty Ltd)

10 9 8 7 6 5 4 3 2 1

Design by Claire Tice and Marley Flory © Penguin Group (Australia)
Photography by Julie Renouf
Food styling by Lee Blaylock
Typeset in Nimbus Sans Novus by Post Pre-press Group, Brisbane, Queensland
Scanning and separations by Splitting Image P/L, Clayton, Victoria
Printed and bound in China by Everbest Printing Co. Ltd

A CIP catalogue record for this book is available from the British Library.

ISBN: 978-1-4053-6324-2

Discover more at www.dk.com